Theme Birthday Parties for Children

Theme Birthday Parties for Children

A Complete Planning Guide

by

ANITA M. SMITH

McFarland & Company, Inc., Publishers
Jefferson, North Carolina, and London

ISBN 0-7864-0743-3 (softcover : 50# alkaline paper) ∞

Library of Congress cataloguing data are available

British Library cataloguing data are available

Cover image ©2000 Artville

Manufactured in the United States of America

*McFarland & Company, Inc., Publishers
Box 611, Jefferson, North Carolina 28640
www.mcfarlandpub.com*

In loving memory of my grandfather,
Ernest Marini, who instilled in me
the importance of hard work
and perserverance.
It was his constant encouragement
and can-do attitude that prompted me
to write and complete this book.

Acknowledgments

Parents of my children's friends have been telling me for years that I should come to their homes and do their children's birthday parties. I decided years ago that I would write a book on the subject instead. When I began, I soon learned that this was not going to be a task accomplished alone.

A great portion of the material from this book is from the help and contributions of my family, my friends, my children's preschool and elementary school teachers, fellow schoolroom moms, PTO members, fellow church youth leaders, camp leaders, and the members and volunteers of my city and museum children's festivals. There are too many to list individually. My sincere thanks goes out to all of you, and thank you for so patiently answering all of my many questions.

Most importantly, I am very grateful to my husband, Hugh, for supporting me during the labor of this book. Without his help, patience, encouragement and *many* ideas this book would never have been written.

I am also very grateful to my children, Tony and Nicole, for their ideas and contributions from a child's perspective. I'm very thankful for their patience with me during my constant writing everywhere we went.

Writing this book while trying to run a household and our restaurant has been a challenge, but we *all* pulled it off. I say all, because without my family's creative input this book would not be complete.

I'd also like to thank my mom, Louise DeRosia, for giving me great parties as a child and for giving me some great ideas for this book. Her creative parties, cakes and piñatas will be forever in my memories.

Many thanks to all of the children who helped in the testing of these parties. Thanks for giving me great memories of you!

Anita M. Smith

Table of Contents

Preface

This book is designed to help you give exciting, fantasy-filled children's birthday parties from start to finish. With the help of this book, you can give your child spectacular birthday parties — parties that can create memories for the whole family to cherish.

As your child anticipates the birthday party that you have created together something special happens between the two (or more) of you. A connection is taking place that you may not even be aware of. The time that you share together planning, baking and playing is time to be treasured. Even something as simple as baking a batch of cupcakes is giving a gift of your love to your child.

It's those little gifts of yourself that are a part of what your child will most cherish when he reaches adulthood. He may not remember that you spent a whole week's salary on the latest popular toy that he had to have, but I assure you, he will remember your cakes and the fun times that you create. I think that the best gift that you can give to your child is the gift of your time.

It is my hope that you will inspire your children to give wonderful parties for their own children. If it weren't for my mother's creativity in planning parties, which gave me such wonderful memories of my own birthday parties as a child, I may not ever have passed on the tradition to my own children.

And I *do* consider it a tradition. I can't imagine what it would be like to be a child who has never experienced the thrill of having a birthday party.

The whole idea behind having a party is spending time with your family and friends, talking, playing, acting silly and just plain having a good time. It's hard for children to interact with one another at a lot of parties nowadays. I find that very sad.

Unfortunately, many of the traditional party games past generations grew up on are being forgotten. Sometimes we just need a little reminder of how we used to play our favorite games as children — a refresher, if you will.

Enjoy your children now; they grow up so fast. The time and effort that you invest in your child's party will give your child memories that will last a lifetime. Plain and simple: It's worth it.

When your friends tell you, months and even years after your child's party is over, that their children are still talking about how much fun they had at your child's party, it will make you feel great — just knowing that all of your effort was appreciated, and that you created memories for not only your children, but other children as well. You'll be amazed at how word gets around the grapevine about your parties, and all of a sudden your friends and neighbors are inspired to have great parties too.

Some chapters in this book use the pronoun "he" and others "she." This is done for simplicity, even when an activity is perfectly suited for both genders.

I have tried to list crafts, games, and activities that can be used either indoors or outdoors for each party theme. There are probably many more ideas for each party theme than you could ever possibly use, to give you several options from which to choose.

For the most part, the crafts, games, activities, and food ideas are uncomplicated. Many of them have been around for years, some for centuries; others will be new to you, but all are kid tested.

Many of the materials needed are materials that you may already have around your home. When necessary, I have given suggestions as to where you can buy those you may not have. For most crafts, games and activities, I have listed what materials you will need, separate from the directions. This will enable you to see at a glance *exactly* what is needed.

I wish you lots of success in all of your party planning! Read the following planning hints and tips, and your party is sure to be a piece of cake!

Introduction: From Planning to Thank-You Notes

🎉 PLANNING 🎉

Involve the birthday child and siblings in the planning — remember that this is *your child's* special day. Your child should be the one to decide which theme he wants. If he wants a sports theme three years in a row, so be it. Chances are your child will choose his latest interest. Maybe a movie or television show has sparked his imagination.

Resist the temptation to sway him into having a theme that *you* may want but he does not. You'd be surprised at what children remember and hold against you twenty years down the road. It may not be worth the argument.

Your child obviously can't make

all of the decisions, but the planning process is about compromise. Your child may want to invite 30 children, but your budget won't allow it — not to mention the fact that 30 children are probably more than you can or want to handle.

Your child, of course, must understand that it is not possible. You may have to explain to him that only his closest friends can come.

Having a theme of course is not a must, but it sure can make a party a lot more fun. Once you and your child have agreed on a party theme, your creative ideas will just snowball, probably leading to more material than you need or even have time for.

Sit down with your child and discuss the crafts, activities, and games — even try them out. Between

3

the two (or more) of you, you're sure to come up with a great party plan.

Planning and testing the games is a lot of fun, if you include the whole family. Siblings and spouses may have great ideas that never crossed your mind. Perhaps the ideas listed in this book will help spark all of your imaginations and encourage you to come up with some fantastic new ideas of your own.

Even at a young age, the birthday child and siblings will feel more excited about the party if they are involved with the preparations. For preschool children that might include something as simple and quick as asking them if they would like to help put a few strips of papier-mâché on a piñata. They will feel that they helped make it. Therefore, the piñata will seem more special to them. An elementary school aged child might get a kick out of making decorations for the house. Let the child do as much as he is capable of doing.

If your child tells you that his friends are too big for a certain game, or that his friends won't eat a certain type of food, it is probably wise to believe him. Your child may know more than you about his friends' likes and dislikes.

One year my daughter's class had an Easter party at school, and one of the moms made the cutest little Easter basket cupcakes with green colored flaked coconut on the top for grass. Every child picked it off. I felt so sorry for that mom. She put so much work into those cupcakes, only to have them picked apart.

Just as I was thinking this, her child said to her, "See, Mom, *I told you* they wouldn't eat it." If only that mom had listened to her child she would have saved herself time, effort, and money.

So listen to your child's advice. He may be wrong and he may be right; just use your best judgment. Oh, by the way, you will notice that I do not use flaked coconut in any of my cake recipes. I definitely learned a lesson that day.

I cannot overemphasize the importance of budgeting your time. Great, memorable, fun parties are *well-planned* parties. If you are anything like me, some days you are just full of energy and other days you're exhausted. On your energetic days you may want to get a lot done. Make sure that you give yourself plenty of time for preparation so that you will not feel rushed.

If you begin planning 1 to 2 months in advance you will feel rested and very calm the day of the party. In my household it seems like it never fails: I'll have my day planned out perfectly and something always seems to interfere with my plans. Beginning early allows time for those unavoidable interruptions.

One way to save time is by buying things a little bit at a time. If you are out shopping and you just happen to see something that fits the theme perfectly, buy it. Save yourself the time of having to go back to the store the day before the party only to find out the store no longer carries that item. You can always save your receipt and return the item if you change your mind.

One of my favorite ways to buy for a party inexpensively and stress-free is through mail order novelty catalogues. I have listed the names of some under the "Party Favors" heading.

♟ HELPFUL ♟ PLANNING TIPS

- Always keep a shopping list with you of the items that you will need to purchase. Keep another copy of the list at home, just in case you lose your other list. I know this may sound unnecessary, but trust me — I've lost a few, and wracked my brain trying to remember what was on the missing list.

- Keep a list of the things that you need to do, and cross them off as they are completed.

- Some toy stores such as Toys "Я" Us have a gift registry service. You might save yourself the hassle of returning gifts by registering at a toy or department store. Try to keep your list realistic and within most people's budgets. I think that this service is a great idea. I always feel a little uncomfortable when the parents of the children invited call and ask, "What does your child want?" I feel put on the spot.

  When I give parties for my children I never think about what gifts my children will receive. I'm more concerned about the ones that I want to give to my guests. I want to make my guests happy and show them a great time. So, if you feel like I do, maybe simply putting a note on the invitation of where your child is registered will help some.

- Avoid scheduling your housecleaning for the day before a party. You will be busy doing other things and will find yourself unrested the day of the party. I like to clean my house anywhere from 2 to 5 days before. That way I'm not frazzled the day before the party. If necessary, just do light touch-up cleaning the day before the party. Children who are old enough to help you out should do so, even the birthday child.

- To keep all of your party supplies organized and out of your way so that you don't find yourself tripping over them, place them in three separate boxes or paper grocery bags. Use one box or bag for decorations; one for games, activities and crafts; and another for your tableware (e.g., plates, cups, napkins, tablecloth, forks and spoons) and non-refrigerated food items. This will help you out *tremendously* the day of the party. Keep these bags and boxes out of your way in a closet or laundry room. Tell your family that the food is *not* to be touched.

♟ BUDGETING ♟ YOUR TIME

One to Two Months Before the Party

- Decide on a theme.
- Make a guest list.
- If making a piñata, do it now to allow time for drying.
- Decide which games you will play and which crafts you will make.
- List all of the supplies needed.
- If buying items through mail order, do it now.

Two Weeks Before the Party

- Make or buy invitations.
- Buy stamps, if necessary.
- Mail or hand-deliver the invitations.
- Order cake or make your own and freeze. Cake can be frozen unfrosted. This will make it easier to frost later. If making the cake this far in advance, wrap it well or place in a well-sealed container.
- Buy party supplies.
- Make any party decorations or craft items that will require time.
- Arrange to have someone help you at the party.

One Week Before the Party

- Make any foods that can be frozen.
- Buy film, videotape, batteries, candles, and matches or lighter.
- Practice games and make a schedule of the activities.
- Place items needed for crafts and games in a box or bag ready to use, along with any prizes that you may need for the games.
- Prepare goody bags and wrap any prizes (if you decide to wrap them).

Two to Five Days Before the Party

- Check camera batteries and replace or charge if necessary.
- Get exact guest count. Call guests who haven't responded.
- Get the goody bags ready, fill them, and place them in a box or basket.

- Buy any remaining food for the party.
- Clean house.
- Clean yard, if necessary.

One Day Before the Party

- Childproof home (put away expensive toys, breakables, jewelry, etc.).
- Finish making the cake or pick up from the bakery.
- Prepare any food that can be made ahead, and thaw anything that was frozen.
- Decorate indoors. Do not put up crepe paper and balloons; they will lose their shape overnight.
- Go over any etiquette rules with your child (for example, answering the door, accepting gifts, thanking guests for coming, learning to take turns, and so forth). Practice these things with your child by playing the part of the guest.
- If possible, set the party table.
- Rent any videos (I recommend renting a video only for slumber parties).
- Find time to relax. Take a bubble bath, or rent a movie related to your theme and watch it with your family.

The Day of the Party

- Bring out all of the party supplies that you have stored.
- Finish preparing any food.
- Decorate outside, if necessary.
- Hang balloons and crepe paper.
- Get cameras and film out.
- Keep party scheduie handy.

- Place out any craft materials that the children will need.

- Check to see that the bathroom is clean and has toilet paper, soap and towels. If the children are older or any moms will be staying, have some feminine supplies handy under the counter.

- Again, stress politeness and briefly go over etiquette rules with family members.

- Enjoy yourself and keep a good sense of humor!

⛄ BUDGET ⛄

None of the parties that I have given have cost me a lot of money. Some of the best parties are very inexpensive.

If your budget is tight, make as much as you can on your own. Make homemade decorations, cake, banners, invitations; buy things on clearance, and make homemade party favors.

Keep an eye out all of the time for bargains and items on clearance sale. This way not only will you find a lot more for your money, but by the time the party arrives you might have all of your shopping out of the way.

I even keep a sharp eye out for items to give as presents for birthday parties that my children may get invited to. We put these into a bag in the closet, which we call "the Birthday Bag." When my children receive a birthday invitation, they get to go "shopping" in the birthday bag, stress-free.

You cannot imagine the time that bag has saved me! It is especially helpful when we get last minute birthday invitations from friends (which happens to us quite often) and there is no time to go shopping. Toy stores put great stuff on clearance to make room for new items year 'round.

Recycle items from around your house for decorations and crafts. Don't throw away crepe paper streamers after the party is over. Roll them back up and save them for another party. I still have rolls from my son's first birthday. That was a long time ago and they still look great.

Save anything that you could use again whether you think you will or not. You just never know. For example, a picture of a parrot or a palm tree that you worked hard on for a Pirate Party may be used again for a Hawaiian Luau Party, or a witches' cauldron that you bought for Halloween could be used as a leprechaun's pot for a St. Patrick's Party.

Throw all of these things in a box marked "Birthday Party Decorations" and put the box in an attic (if you feel that the weather won't damage it), basement or closet to keep it out of your way until the next party.

A woman once told me that all of the people where she lived had major blowout parties for their children. The average cost was three times what I usually spend. I really don't see the purpose in this practice at all. The children aren't going to care about what you spend. They are going to be more interested in what a great time they have, and showing your guests a great time shouldn't put you in the poorhouse.

Please try to keep in mind that your child's party is not meant to impress other parents. It is not meant to outdo your neighbor's last party. It is for the *children*. It's about making great memories to be cherished!

🎉 GUEST LIST 🎉

When making a guest list, consider whether the party will be indoors or outdoors. If it must be indoors, keep the list small.

Consider how much room you will have if the weather changes your plans for an outdoor party. Do you have a basement or garage that you can set the party up in? Keep an eye on the weather forecast.

Always be sure to have at least one adult or teenager to help you during the party. A spouse, grandparent, relative, friend, neighbor, even an ex-spouse, all are considerations for helpers. Older siblings who may feel too old to be one of the party participants may feel important if they can help give the party. Reward them somehow, if you like.

If you intend on having a large group of guests, you will need more than one helper. When having a party with children 5 and under, it might be wise to have one adult per every 4–5 children. For parties with children 6 and up you will need one adult per every 8–9 children.

If the party is for young children, say 4 and under, write on the invitation that parents are welcome to stay if they want. Some parents may feel more comfortable staying than dropping off such a young child. They may even like getting ideas from you, if they have never given a birthday party before.

I am not partial to very large parties. I feel it is best to keep the list small. Any party with over 20 children will likely end up being total chaos. It may be best to have two separate parties — one for family such as cousins, aunts, uncles and grandparents, and one for friends and neighbors.

The following is just a guide to help you plan how many guests to invite and the length the party should be for each particular age group:

3–4 Year Olds

Number of guests: up to 6
Length of party: 1½–2 hours
Children of this age tire easily. Remember not to plan a party for this age group around naptime. Plan a bathroom break, since many children of this age will forget to go.

5 Year Olds

Number of guests: up to 8
Length of party: 2 hours
Children of this age tend to be a bit selfish. They have difficulty understanding winning and losing, so try to keep the games less competitive. Children of this age still tire easily and still require a bathroom break.

6 Year Olds

Number of guests: 10–12
Length of party: 2–2½ hours
Children of this age are very energetic, and tend to have short attention spans. Some still have difficulty sharing and have short emotional fuses. Parties for this age group should be well organized.

7 Year Olds

Number of guests: 10–15
Length of party: 2–2½ hours
Children of this age are still very energetic, but calmer than the 6 year olds. They need activities of short duration, perhaps no more than 10 minutes. Use a variety of activities with this age.

8–9 Year Olds

Number of guests: 10–20
Length of party: 2–3 hours
Children of this age may, on first arriving, think that they are too old to play party games — that is, until they have played them. Then they leave begging for more. Games go quickly with children in this age group, so plan plenty of them.

10–11 Year Olds

Number of guests: 10–20
Length of party: 2–3 hours
Children of this age group are beginning to understand and really enjoy theme parties. Games go quickly with children in this age group. To keep them busy, plan a few more than you think you will need. They will be thrilled to play them.

🎉 INVITATIONS 🎉

When you invite a guest, it is best done with a written invitation. Calling a guest a few days before a party has its drawbacks. First of all, it puts the parent that you are calling on the spot to come up with an answer, and that parent may not know what a spouse or other family members have planned for the day of your party. The parent may need to discuss it with the family. He or she may not even know if the child *wants* to go.

Furthermore, when you call a parent a few days before the party — which has happened to me numerous times — it leaves the parent wondering if his or her child was invited because other children could not come. They will get the feeling that their child was invited as a fill-in. You really don't want your guests to feel that they were a last-minute thought.

Another good reason to send a written invitation is that it serves as a visual reminder of the party. Having it sitting on the counter or stuck to the refrigerator reminds the parents all week that the party is coming up, so they won't forget to come. So unless some unusual circumstance prevents you from getting the invitations out on time, written invitations are really the best bet.

But don't plan on letting your child bring the invitations to school to pass them out. A classmate who has not been invited may not understand the fact that you have a budget to follow. Hurt feelings are the likely result. The only exception to this would be if you were to invite the entire class. But as a general rule it is best to mail or hand deliver the invitations to the guest's home.

Another reason not to pass the invitations out at school is because they may never reach the parent of the child invited. Many children tend to be forgetful. One year my son gave an invitation to one of his good friends, who forgot to give the invitation to his mom, and she didn't find out about the party until it was over. She found the invitation buried in his school bookbag days after the party. My children's school has a student directory, but this particular child had an unlisted number, so we couldn't call him. It would have been better if we had just delivered the invitation to his home, or asked him for his address.

All of the party themes in this book include ideas for making invitations by hand, but if you are short on time, make the invitations on a computer, if you have one. If you don't have a computer, see if a friend or relative will allow you to use theirs. You can use all of the wording from this book and simply pull up a picture on the computer that goes with your theme.

Some stores specialize in personalized invitations. Although they are nice they can be quite expensive. Most discount stores, card shops, pharmacies, and party supply stores sell ready-made invitations at a reasonable price, although few of them are very personal.

If you will be hand-delivering your invitations, you can make them out of recycled materials such as cardboard, toilet paper tubes, drink bottles, etc. Jazz up a paper invitation with glitter glue, stickers, stamps or stencils.

State the following information on the invitation:

- The fact that this is a birthday party.
- The first and last name of the birthday child.
- Date and (for outdoor parties) rain date.

- Exact time the party will begin and end.
- Place and address (include a map).
- Your home phone number (and work number, if you like).
- Whether a meal is to be served.
- Whether guests are to wear a certain type of clothing (e.g., costume, play clothes, bathing suit).

Write on the invitation when you will need a response by, so that you will know in advance how many children will be coming to the party. This will allow enough time to order cake, buy any extra party favors, obtain extra seats, etc.

Many people will misplace the invitation or forget to call you. Call them, if they haven't called you. That way you won't be left wondering how many people to plan for.

Always include a map to your home or the place of the party. I have one map that I have used for years. Every time I have a party, I just run copies of it. If you don't have a copier at home, take your map to a copy center, office supply store, or your local library and make copies there.

If your child has a friend whose birthday is near his own, check with the parent of that child and find out what day they plan to have a party. There is nothing worse than planning a party for a specific day for weeks, and then receiving an invitation in the mail from one of your child's closest friends for a party on the same day — or worse yet, at the same time!

One year that happened to us. All of my child's friends who were invited to his party were also invited to his classmate's party. I discussed it with the other mom and decided to switch my date, since she had had reservations for weeks at a local farm. We called everyone we had invited and changed the date. Otherwise everyone would have had to make a difficult choice between which party to attend, and lots of hurt feelings and disappointment could have been the result.

Both parties turned out great and *everyone* was able to attend. (I'm especially glad that I was able to attend the other party, since it was a great source of ideas and information for the Barnyard Party!)

🎉 PHONE 🎉 ETIQUETTE

Keep your invited guest list near the phone, along with a pen. Remind everyone in your household to write down "yes" or "no" next to each guest's name when that guest calls to respond to the invitation.

Role-playing is a good way to practice having your child take phone messages. For instance, have your child pick up one phone extension while you pick up another. Dictate a brief message and phone number, and have your child write the information on a pad of paper.

Go over general telephone rules with your child. Explain to him that he should never leave someone waiting for too long, and teach him not to yell into the receiver.

🎉 HIRING 🎉 ENTERTAINMENT

I have talked to many people who have hired clowns, puppeteers, magicians, and so forth, and they have all had good experiences. They all found out about the people that they hired through seeing them at other parties. If you plan to hire entertainment, ask for references, and ask if you can see them perform at another party before hiring them.

If you have Internet access from your home, a friend, a relative, or a local library, check there to see what type of hired entertainment is available in your area. Use "party planning" as your keywords. Some cities have an amazing selection for children's birthday party entertainment.

Plan on having the entertainment arrive about 30 minutes after the party begins. This will allow the children time to get to know one another, talk and play. Try to fit in one or two games if possible.

Make sure that the entertainment fits the age group of party guests. My daughter once went to a party where there was a clown magician. The children were all about 4 years old, with the exception of two older children. The clown was very good and had some great jokes and tricks, but the younger children just didn't get any of them. That very same party was supposed to be a dress-up party. The two themes (clown magician and dress up) just didn't work well together.

We searched high and low for an outfit for my daughter to wear to the party. She got all dressed up and was eager to get to the party thinking that they were going to do girlie things like using make-up and perfume. Instead she sat around watching a clown for an hour. Although she enjoyed the clown, she came home a bit disappointed.

My point is this: Make sure that the hired entertainment fits any planned theme, that it is appropriate to the age group of the guests, and that it is *entertaining.*

🎉 DECORATIONS 🎉

A variety of birthday decorations can be purchased at most department stores, card shops, party supply stores, grocery stores, and even craft stores. Try to use colors and decorations that fit the theme when possible. Each party chapter in this book lists decorating ideas related to the theme, but here I will just touch on a few general ideas.

Purchase crepe paper and hang it over your front door, from a mailbox, from a lamppost (away from the heat of the lamp), from your front porch, from a tree, over the party table, from chairs or whatever comes to mind. Roll up and save what you can after the party.

Use balloons in the same manner as crepe paper — that is, put them everywhere! Rub balloons against your clothing to statically charge them and make them stick to the wall or ceiling. You can purchase cans of helium from the party supply department in some stores, or you can rent tanks of helium from party rental shops and from welding shops. To make a cluster of balloons, blow up 10-12 balloons and tie a string to one, use masking tape to stick

the balloons together, and hang from the string.

Put decorations on the front door, inside doors, on garage doors, and on walls, windows, fences, trees, and so forth. You can make your own decorations out of cardboard or construction paper. You can print them from your computer, or even use colored coloring book pages.

Make a long "Happy Birthday" banner on your computer. Banners printed on a laser printer will require banner paper, and banners printed on a dot matrix printer will require the standard continuous sheets of paper.

If you need a large sheet of paper, check with your local newspaper to see if they will sell you something called "end roll paper." This makes for a great banner. Also good for banners are the long sheets of packing paper many mail order companies use. Large sheets of paper can also be purchased at paper goods stores.

For parties that must be held in the garage, put away any tools and make sure that nothing can fall onto anyone if it should be bumped. Hang clean drop cloths (such as painters use) or old sheets from the ceiling to cover tools. Decorations can be hung from the drop cloths or old sheets by taping or pinning them on.

If your party is going to be held in a backyard, you may want to put a sign on the garage door, front door, or fence directing your guests to go the backyard. It could read, "Megan's party this way" or "Please meet us in the backyard for Jason's Party."

You could even put a sign out at the road that leads to your house, if it is easy to miss. I have seen some real eye catchers that are made of bright posterboard and decorated with balloons and curled ribbon.

For a centerpiece on the party table, you may be able to find commercial paper centerpieces to fit the occasion — or you can use a stuffed animal, toys, hats, buckets or baskets that go with the theme.

Hang decorations indoors the night before the party, so that you will not need to worry about them the day of the party. (The exception is balloons and crepe paper, which will lose their shape if hung too early.) Do this while the birthday child is in bed asleep; otherwise he will be too excited to fall asleep. When he wakes up he will be very thrilled to see the house decorated. The morning of the party, or a couple of hours before the party, you will want to finish doing your decorations indoors and outdoors.

In the party chapters I have listed suggested songs under the "Decorations" heading, because I feel that music, like decorations, adds to the mood or excitement of a theme party. Music tends to relax the children, especially when some of the guests do not know one another. Many children have no problem breaking into a spur of the moment dance when a great song comes on.

I have listed a variety of songs that fit each theme, but don't go rushing out to buy a bunch of recordings just because they are suggested. They are listed just in case you or someone you know has these songs that you can play, and just in case you may have overlooked the idea.

Many of these songs are classics and have stood the test of time. Some your children may love; some they may think are "old." Let them listen to the songs and choose what they think is best. Call local radio stations to request songs, and listen to them before deciding which songs to buy to help keep costs down. You may even be able to find some of them at your local library.

Many used record, tape and CD stores have great recordings — old and new — at reasonable prices. Some secondhand stores also have a huge selection to choose from. They tend to carry recordings that the department stores don't have room for.

One thing that I like to do before a party is go through my entire collection of music looking for songs that fit the theme. I narrow it down to several choices, then I ask my children which they like. I put all of the songs that my family and I agree on onto one tape, which we play during the party.

Guests often ask me where I buy such great recordings to fit each theme. They are usually surprised when I tell them that they were from my own collection of songs. Even if you have a small collection, you'll be amazed how many songs you probably already have around your home that fit the theme.

🎉 FOOD 🎉

Whenever possible, I like to feed my guests shortly after everyone has arrived and played a game or two. Some guests may arrive hungry or thirsty. Try not to make them wait until the end of the party to eat, even if it is just cake and ice cream that you are serving.

Try not to serve cake and ice cream just before sending guests home near dinnertime. It's annoying to a parent who has just worked hard on dinner to have a child come home stuffed on desserts. Besides, it is nice to get the food part out of the way. Once that is done you'll feel free to play, relax and just enjoy the day.

Keep the menu as simple as possible. You won't have the time for an elaborate meal, and the children certainly won't expect one. All of the themes in this book have meal ideas, but if you just don't have the time to prepare anything, let the children make their own food. Set out a tray of sandwich meat, cheeses, bread and condiments, and let guests help themselves. Children love to make their own food anyway. It's more fun for them to eat something that they created.

Pizza ordered from a local pizzeria also goes over well. I'd recommend ordering some with just cheese and some with pepperoni. Figure 2-3 average size pieces for each child. Don't forget to save room for cake and ice cream!

Some children may be allergic to dairy products, so you might want to have an alternative food handy for them. For a child who can't have ice cream, offer a popsicle instead. If your child is allergic to cake, serve pie instead. Who says that you can't put candles on a pie? If you want to be different, so be it.

If the weather is warm and cooperative, I strongly suggest eating outdoors. Food somehow always seems to taste better outdoors, and you won't have to worry over spilled drinks or crumbs on the floor.

If you don't already have a picnic table, consider purchasing or making one. It's a great investment. I have used my picnic table (which seats 12) more

times than I can count, and not just for parties. My children and their friends always seem to gravitate toward the picnic table for long chats, invention building, crafts creations, or relief from the hot sun (our table sits under a large oak tree), and it makes a great pretend pirate ship or bus.

If you will be taking your party on the road, remember to purchase ice to keep foods at a safe temperature. Meats and dairy products can spoil quite quickly and cause harmful bacteria to grow. Besides, there is nothing like an ice cold drink straight out of the cooler after a hard day of playing. Pack a thermos of hot cocoa on a cold day.

A little hint: Serve drinks without caffeine in them. Some children just can't handle it as well as others. Check the labels on beverages. It's not just colas that have caffeine.

When you have a party with a lot of children, drinks tend to get mixed up. To help identify whose drink is whose, write each child's name on his cup. Another way for children to identify their cups is by giving each child a different colored soda straw.

🎉 CAKE 🎉

How much cake? That's always the big question. The way I see it, it's better to have a little too much than not enough. In our house if there isn't any leftover cake after the party we are disappointed. I take it as a compliment when the guests devour it, but I'd also like to have some.

I've noticed that as my children's friends get bigger, so do their appetites.

So, I have been baking two batches of cake mix, sometimes using my 10 × 16 inch broiler pan for rectangular cakes, instead of a 9 × 13 inch pan. For small parties with young children, one box of cake mix should be enough.

If you are having a party with 12 or more children all around 9–12 years old, play it safe and bake two batches, even if you just make the second batch simple cupcakes.

Baking and freezing the cake one week or more in advance can save you time during the week of the party. Freezing it for even just 45 minutes can make the frosting go on much easier.

Tools for decorating cakes can be found in most craft stores, kitchen supply stores and department stores. You will need a couple of decorating bags and basic frosting tips. Nothing fancy or out of the ordinary is needed for the cake recipes in this book.

Making the cakes is easy, but it does require time. Trust me: If I can do it, you can too. Each year you will get better at it. The results will surprise you, even make you a bit proud of your accomplishment.

One thing to remember before you begin frosting the cake is to gently wipe away any loose crumbs from the surface. This prevents the crumbs from getting into the frosting. For cakes that require a smooth surface, pipe rows of frosting in the correct area, then spread with a metal frosting spatula or a smooth knife. When using a star tip to create a design, surface crumbs are rarely a problem. (I love my star tip, but unfortunately I can't use it on every cake.) When using a star tip, remember to keep the stars close together, otherwise the cake will show

through. I freeze any leftover frosting for another cake.

What should you set the cake on? If you do not have a platter large enough to hold your cake, cover a large heavy piece of cardboard, the backside of a cookie sheet, or even a cutting board with aluminum foil. Tape it on the underside with masking tape. If desired, cover the foil with colored plastic wrap for added flair. Use green for a grass effect, blue for a water or sky effect, and so on.

If it would make you feel more at ease about decorating for a first time, take a course in cake decorating. Check with your local craft store, kitchen supply store or community college to see if they offer courses in cake decorating.

🎉 ICE CREAM 🎉

Cost wise, you can't beat a store brand carton of ice cream, and the children will love it. Some people choose to purchase individual plastic cups of ice cream for parties because they are so easy, but they can be expensive.

If you have the time, you can make ice cream creations or ice cream cones ahead of time. They are just as convenient to serve as the cups, and you can get very creative. Place ice cream balls on cupcake liners and decorate with pieces of candy, licorice, sprinkles, chocolate chips, icing, and cherries. You can even make them into "heads" with funny faces. Set them on top of a cookie sheet or in a pan, cover with plastic wrap and refreeze until needed.

The children get a big thrill out of

this, and it saves you the hassle of having to scoop ice cream during the party. All you do is pass them out. Another advantage is that kids usually realize that one ice cream ball or cone is a complete serving. When the cones are gone you won't have anyone asking for seconds or thirds, the way you might if you were scooping from a carton.

You could even set out a variety of different toppings and let children decorate their scoops by themselves.

🎉 PLACE CARDS 🎉

Many people no longer use place cards at birthday parties, but I feel that clearly marking where each child is to be seated is very important. I didn't realize the importance of place cards until one time when I forgot to make them. When it came time to eat, my daughter did not get to sit near her two best friends. It saddened them all, and her friends got stuck sitting near children they did not know. I could sense that her friends were a little uncomfortable sitting near two rowdy boys. I didn't want to cause any hurt feelings by moving the children who were seated near my daughter, so I just left things as they were — but I knew my daughter was disappointed.

You may use place cards to keep rowdy children separated, or to keep very shy children near someone that they will feel comfortable with. I usually place all of the children who know each other from school on one side of the table. I place all of the children who know each other from our neighborhood on the other side. This always works well, and everyone is happy.

The following are a few place card suggestions:

- Before the party, write each guest's name on a sheet of paper. Tape the sheets of paper to the party table where you would like each guest to be seated. Place a container of crayons on the table. As the guests arrive, ask them to sit where they find their names. Tell them that they may draw a picture of anything that they like, or have them draw a picture that relates to the party theme. This will keep everyone busy until all of the guests have arrived. It may even help break the ice among children who don't know each other well. To help them feel more comfortable, talk to them about their pictures.

- Before the party, fill balloons with small favors such as gum, candy, barrettes, rings, necklaces, or plastic figures. If desired, fill balloons with helium before tying closed. Write each child's name on a balloon with paint or felt tip marker. Tie a string to each balloon and attach to the back of each child's chair. Pop open the balloon, and surprise!

- Attach a large bow or store-bought helium filled birthday balloon to the birthday child's chair.

- Purchase tiny baskets or nut cups. These can be found at party supply stores. Label them with each child's name. Fill with gumdrops, candy or peanuts. If desired, wrap each basket or cup with colored cellophane or tissue paper. Tie with a ribbon. You could even put a nametag on the ribbon.

- Personalize favors such as plastic buckets, barrettes, bookmarks, or bottles of blowing bubbles.

- Take a Polaroid picture of each guest as he or she arrives. Write each child's name on the white part, and place at the table where the child is to be seated.

⚲ ARRIVAL ⚲ OF GUESTS

If you are playing theme songs, play them as guests will be arriving. A good place to set up the music might be on a front porch, by the door. This helps the guests get into the spirit as they arrive.

Always introduce yourself to any child or parent who does not know you. Offer a handshake and a cheerful "Hello, nice to meet you. I am _____'s mom/dad." Introduce the guests and parents to one another. Take guests' coats and place them out of the way, but let them know where to find them. Remind your family to politely take the presents and place them all in one spot out of reach from curious little hands.

Expect some guests to arrive early. Don't be surprised when the first one arrives 20 minutes before the party is supposed to begin and you are still hanging crepe paper and balloons. It happens! Not often, but it happens. Some will show up 20 minutes late.

So, plan for early and late arrivals before you begin the party. Start out with a craft, or have the children draw their own placemats while waiting for other guests to arrive.

Keep in mind, too, that occasionally a guest who said he would come never shows. Don't hold up the beginning of the party for too long, waiting for a guest who may never arrive.

You will want to start the party out as calmly as possible. Some children may be scared or unsure about staying if the house is in chaos and children are running around screaming and yelling. It doesn't have to be that way, and won't be if you plan well.

Assure the parents that their child will have a good time, if they are leaving their child with you. Invite the parent to stay, if you want them to.

As the guests are arriving it is very helpful, and actually necessary, to have two people running the party. One will be kept busy greeting the children and parents. The other will need to keep the children who already have arrived occupied. You may spend the first half-hour just greeting guests. Your helper can make sure that the children are introduced to one another and that each one receives a nametag; then the helper can start them on a craft or activity.

Occasionally an adult with the gift of gab just won't let you get to your other guests. It may be necessary to cut the conversation short and excuse yourself. You may tell your helper before the party to help you out with this type of situation, if it should occur, by somehow "rescuing" you.

In such situations my husband usually calls me to come and help him with a craft or something, and I then say, "Well, I'd better go, please excuse me. I'll see you at 2:00." I then privately thank my husband (sometimes a look of relief is all it takes for him to know that he has just saved the day).

If a parent is staying, immediately put him or her to work. Let that parent help you out. This is a party for the children, and if you get stuck talking, things may not run smoothly. So by all means put parents to work, or just let them watch the party.

One way for the children to feel welcomed, and for the children to re-member one another's names, is to an-nounce their arrival: "Hey everyone, Josh is here! Everyone say, 'Hi, Josh!'" Everyone then yells loudly, "Hi, Josh!" and Josh usually walks in beaming, be-cause he feels a bit special right from the get-go.

☙ NAMETAGS ☙

Nametags are very helpful when guests don't know one another. You can purchase nametag or name badge stick-ers at office supply stores, paper goods stores or party supply stores. You can even make some out of construction paper to fit the party theme. If you have a computer, try printing some on it.

☙ SCHEDULE ☙

Make a step-by-step schedule showing each stage of the party and things are sure to go much smoother. Use a pen or highlighter and cross off each thing as you finish. Keep the schedule on a clipboard or in your pocket during outdoor parties so that it doesn't blow away. The following is an example of a schedule.

11:00–11:20	Guests arrive and draw placemats.
11:20–11:35	Plant Magic Beanstalks.
11:35–11:45	Play Cup Stacking Con-test.
11:45–12:00	Have children go to the bathroom and wash hands.
12:00–12:20	Eat lunch.
12:20–12:30	Take kids in front yard and play Beanbag Toss, while someone hides the "gold."
12:30–12:35	Take a picture of all of the kids on the front steps.
12:35–12:45	Begin Hunt for the Giant's Gold.
12:45–1:00	Play Know Your Beans.
1:00–1:20	Cake and ice cream.
1:20–1:40	Open presents.
1:40–1:50	Play Guess the Number of Beans.
1:50–2:00	Pass out goody bags and Magic Beanstalks.

Extra games in case we have time: Magic Hen Relay Race, Jack and the Beanstalk Charades and Bean Bingo.

This schedule, of course, is just an example. You may choose to only have a two-hour party. You may or may not be up to doing a lot of games. If neces-sary, write a brief description on how to play each game next to it on your list. Always have some extra games planned. Some games may go faster than you had planned, leaving you with unplanned time and restless guests.

♟ PICTURES ♟

Preserve your party memories forever with photos and videos. Before the day of the party, check your camera and video camera. Make sure the batteries are new or charged, check the flash, and buy some film.

Take plenty of pictures through all stages of the party. I feel that you or someone you trust should do the picture taking. It only takes a moment to get a picture, then put the camera down and continue with what your doing. If you have someone else take the pictures, be specific as to what you want pictures of.

One year I made the mistake of handing my camera to a mother who stayed at the party. I wasn't specific as to how many pictures of the kids breaking the piñata I wanted, so she took one of each child. She took an entire roll of film on one game and we had no more film left for the rest of the party. I was so disappointed. I never even got a picture of my daughter with her cake or with her friends.

If you like, have duplicate pictures made of the party, and send one to each guest with a thank you note. Make sure that the picture that you send to each child includes that child in the picture.

Use your video camera if you have one, or rent one from a camera store or video rental store. Someone that you are close to may let you borrow theirs.

When taking videos of the party, it is great to take advantage of certain situations. For example, while you have all of the children lined up for a game, put the camera on each child and have them say their name. This way you will

remember them forever. People change, and without this little memory aid you may not remember who was who.

During the opening of the gifts, try to be on the opposite side of the circle of each child that hands the gift to the birthday child. If you are videotaping from this angle, you will have a shot of the face that goes with each gift given. After the party, this will help you when writing thank you notes.

If you have close relatives or friends who live too far away to attend your child's party, and wish they could be there, make a video of the big day and send it to them. If they sent a present, be sure to videotape your child opening the present. Your child could personally thank them for it on film. Send the tape along with a note from your child. If he is too young to write, send a picture that he has drawn. Include other special events on the video.

It would also be a great idea to send grandparents any doubles of your photos. Not only would they enjoy looking at them, but it's also a good idea for someone else to have copies of your family photos just in case something should happen to your own. No one likes to think about the possibility of a fire, flood, tornado, or hurricane, but it is a good idea to be safe — just in case. Besides, sending copies to grandparents just plain makes them happy, and shows them that you care.

♟ CRAFTS ♟

Begin saving any materials, such as recycled items, well in advance. If you don't think that you can save enough materials before the day of the party, ask friends or relatives if they could save some for you. Restaurants and local businesses may even be able to give you many items that you need. Save cardboard from the packaging of items (backs of tablet paper, shirt inserts, cereal boxes, etc.). Save scrap material from sewing projects or household repairs (lace, ribbons, cloth, wallpaper, wood).

I think that it is a good idea to try out craft projects before the day of the party. One reason is so that you can show the children a sample of the finished piece, making it easier for them to comprehend. The other reason is to know *exactly* how to do the project before the day of the party, making it easier for you to explain.

Forewarn the parents on the invitation if you plan on doing messy craft projects. Tell them to have their children wear old playclothes so that a nice new outfit doesn't get ruined. When doing craft projects roll up the children's sleeves to protect them.

Crafts should be done at the beginning of the party to allow drying time, and also because not all guests arrive at the same time, making it difficult to begin playing games. Be sure to write the children's names on their craft projects to prevent any confusion.

🎉 GAMES AND 🎉 ACTIVITIES

I feel that playing games is one of the most important parts of a party.

During game playing children learn about fair play, sportsmanship and the values of working together in a group. I believe that it can be an important learning experience.

The children, of course, think that playing games is important because it is fun! A party just isn't any fun without games. Ask any child and they are sure to agree.

For each party described in this book, I have listed quite a few games. Time won't allow you to play all of the games listed under the party theme, so you and your child will need to pick the ones that you like best.

You may want to try out some games before the party to see which ones you like and to get an idea of how long each one will take. How many games you plan will depend on a few things: How old are the children? How long will it take them to play? How long will the party last?

Always plan for more games than you think you will need. It's an unpleasant surprise to find there is 1 hour left before the party is over and you're out of ideas, stuck with some bored children on your hands asking, "What's next?"

Let your "extra" games be ones that don't require making, constructing or buying items. Then you won't unnecessarily waste your time or money on a game that you may not have time to play. List these extra games on the bottom or back of your schedule.

If you find that you haven't planned enough games, you can also play the most successful games again. For some reason, at every party you will have one game that the children can't seem to get enough of.

If some children finish eating

before others, and get restless waiting on them, have your helper keep them busy playing a previous game. One good example is to let the children practice roping the steer head during the Wild West Party. Another good example would be to let the faster eaters practice throwing their paper airplanes during the Airplane Party. Keep them busy with something that won't distract the children who are still eating.

Try to plan both active and quiet games. It's a party, so make your opening game a good one. Once they've played some games and worked up an appetite, then feed them. After they have eaten, you'll want to play calm games. Remember they are all full, so it may not be a good idea to have them running around yet. Give their food a chance to digest, especially if it is hot out.

It is a good idea to plan some indoor games even if your party is going to be held outdoors. Hopefully you won't have to worry about it rainin' on your parade, but better to be safe than sorry.

If all of the children attending the party are roughly equal in physical and mental abilities, have a drawing to choose teams. Before the party, paint just the tips of popsicle sticks. Paint equal amounts of two different colors. Place the painted tips down inside of a cup so that no one can see them. Have each child draw a stick. The color that they draw determines which team they are on. This same method may also be used with folded paper slips stuck into a hat. Write "team 1" on half of the slips and "team 2" on the other half.

If you will be having a mixture of preschoolers and elementary school aged children, it is especially important to choose teams carefully to make them "even" in abilities. In this case, an adult will need to choose who goes on what team. If you have two children larger or smaller than the rest of the children, put them on opposite teams. This way one team will not have an advantage over another team. Try to split the teams equally gender wise also, unless a game specifies boys on one team and girls on another.

When you are short one child to make teams of equal number, a helper or adult should fill in. If we have an unequal amount of children for a game, my husband or I always fill in. For a relay race we may pretend to be slower, so that the other team doesn't get upset and think that their opponents had an advantage over them by having us on their team. On the other hand, as the children get older you won't *have* to pretend. You'll be struggling to keep up with them!

This day belongs to the birthday child, so make sure that he is the first in every activity.

Strongly discourage talk of "winners" or "losers." Keep the competitive spirit to a minimum. If someone wins, fine, but do not allow bragging. Try to play down that a team won or lost. Just move on to the next activity quickly.

I never find hurt feelings a problem at any of my parties, possibly because we move on so quickly from one activity to the next. No one ever gets a moment to brood over losing. Before they know it they're into another game and have won at it.

Nevertheless, with children 5 and under, it may be necessary to avoid prizes for winners. (See next section for more discussion of prizes.)

For games that require a blindfold,

some children 5 and under may become frightened, so just let them close their eyes if they like. For all of the games that require a blindfold, use a clothespin to attach it around the children's heads. This is much easier than tying and untying the blindfold for each child.

Many of the games listed in this book require a clearly marked throwing line, boundary marker or start and finish line. I have used many different things to mark these. My favorite is bright yarn, because it is easily moved and transported in a game bag or game box (what I keep all of my materials in during a party). I also like it because it can be used on grass, cement, or carpet.

I have also used the orange colored sport field cones. These can be purchased at most sporting goods stores and at stores with sporting goods departments. These cones are a small version of the cones road construction crews use. They make great start and finish markers, because they are brightly colored and easy to see. These cones also work well for obstacle courses, slalom courses and soccer goals.

Chalk is best used on cement or blacktop driveways. Masking tape is best used on cement floors, floor tile and linoleum. A few other ideas that all work well on the spur of the moment are boxes, garden hoses, sticks, yardsticks, chairs, door mats, fences, paper plates and pieces of cardboard.

Whenever possible, secure the markers so that the running feet of players cannot dislodge them. Always keep safety in mind when securing any marker. Do not use rocks that a child can fall on and be hurt on. Wires or stakes that poke up are also out of the question.

When planning games or activities, glance through some of the other chapters to see if there may be games under a different theme that you can use. Even if you don't plan on using a central theme, all the chapters have great party ideas.

You may even be able to use many of the games for planning family reunions, neighborhood block parties, church youth group gatherings, school class parties, school or church carnivals, fund raising events, end of the school year field day celebrations, museum/zoo/city children's festivals, themed restaurant events, and more. The possible uses for this book are endless.

🎉 PRIZES 🎉

Whether to award prizes is up to you. Many parties nowadays do not. I really feel that awarding prizes for children 6 and older is a good idea. Prizes add to the fun and excitement of a party. Many of the parties listed have group games, where a whole group is guaranteed to win. You could play a few group games to be sure both teams have a chance to win prizes.

Prizes should not be given at parties with children 5 and under, unless there are older children at the party who will expect them. Many children simply cannot understand losing at this age, and shouldn't be expected to.

If you wish to award prizes to everyone participating in a game, that usually goes over very well. Fill a box with shredded newspaper, mix in some wrapped candies or inexpensive toys, and let the children hunt for their "treasure" in the box after each game.

Children 6 and up should be able to handle the concept of winning and losing. Many of them have been in school long enough to have learned that they aren't always going to get their way.

Still, it's best to make sure that everyone wins a prize, even if you award them for having the "best smile," being the "best helper," being the "most patient," etc. Explain to the children not to worry if they didn't win a prize on a specific game, because everyone will win one. Do this so that they don't get discouraged.

Occasionally you will have a sore loser. Keep a close eye out for facial expressions during the party. If you have an emotional child on your hands, head off any problems beforehand by making sure that child receives a prize. Some children may arrive at the party a little tired, not feeling well; maybe they had a scuffle with a sibling before the party or recently lost a relative. Any number of things can be brewing inside of them. So be aware and patient with emotional children. You just may be the person who brightens their day!

If you want to make sure that everyone wins a prize, but can't remember who has already won a prize, put a sticker on each child as they win. If you see by the end of the party that someone hasn't won yet, award that child a prize. Make sure that they go home feeling good. Other ideas for being awarded a prize are best placemat drawing, having the best manners, eating the most cake, and so forth.

Each party theme in this book has more prize and favor suggestions than

you can possibly buy. They are listed to give you ideas from which to pick and choose. Use the ideas as a guide. Don't go over your budget.

To help keep costs down, recycle some of your child's inexpensive toys. If your child has some toys in brand new condition and no longer needs or wants them, give them as prizes. Kid's meal prizes from restaurants work great.

Have more prizes than you think you will need on hand; you can always put extras away for another party. A game may end in a tie leaving you with two winners and only one prize left. Put all of the prizes in a box and let the children pick out a prize.

Another inexpensive prize idea that goes over very well is candy. Place wrapped pieces of candy and suckers in a bowl or tin can. As each child wins at a game let them pick out a piece of candy.

🎉 OPENING 🎉 THE GIFTS

Before the party, discuss with your child the importance of saying "thank you" after opening each gift.

When opening the gifts, have the children all sit in a large circle. Seat the birthday child in the center of the circle. Pass the presents out to the children giving the presents. If there are two or three siblings giving one present, seat them together.

Begin by choosing one child to go first. He then passes the birthday present to the birthday child in the center. Have the birthday child read the card out loud, or help him read it if he is too young. To some children this is very important. They may have spent a long time making the card.

Let your child open the present, show it to everyone, and say "Thank you" before moving on to have the next child pass his present to the birthday child. Move clockwise from one child to the next.

This arrangement is much better than just having all of the children pushing and shoving to get their present to the birthday child, and trying to see what the presents are. When that happens, it's too chaotic. A lot of times my children come home from a party and I ask, "Did they like the present?" and the typical response is, "I don't know. I couldn't see him open it. There were too many kids pushing and shoving."

That always bothers me. The birthday child usually doesn't even know whom the present came from when the opening is done in that manner. I feel very strongly that the giver of the gift should know that the birthday child appreciates it.

Before the party, discuss with your child how he should react if he receives a gift that he already has. I think that it is best just to say a sincere "Thank you" and move on. The giver may have had high hopes that the birthday child would like the gift and may be very disappointed to learn that the child already has one, so it's best not to mention it.

Place all presents promptly in a large garbage bag or laundry basket, and put this somewhere where prying fingers cannot get to it. I know that may seem selfish, but let's face it: Something is bound to get lost or bro-

ken. It is best to wait until all of the guests have gone home to bring out the presents and play with them. A sibling may feel special if you give him the job of placing the presents where they belong and throwing away any wrapping paper in a nearby paper grocery bag or garbage bag.

An adult may want to write down a list of who has given which gift, or you may videotape the opening of the gifts (see the earlier section on pictures). This is important for you to know who your child should write thank you notes to, and what items to thank them for.

Helpful Tip: If you have a large present to give to your child, and it is too big to wrap with regular wrapping paper, wrap it with a paper tablecloth. You may even be able to find one with "Happy Birthday" written on it.

THINGS MAY NOT BE PERFECT

Don't hold high expectations. The weather may not always be on your side, so be prepared. You may even want to put an alternate rain date on your invitations. If it rains during an outdoor party, bring the party indoors, or into a garage. Sitting and tossing games can be played indoors, or the children can make crafts.

If your child becomes ill, consult your doctor, and if necessary reschedule the party for a time when your child will be feeling better and isn't contagious to others. Call your guests as soon as possible.

If you will be holding the party at a place that requires the children to come with a permission slip, such as at a horseback riding stable, have extras on hand. Someone is bound to show up without one.

There will always be that one "difficult" child. I've never had a party yet without one. He may need special attention, or he may be looking for it. I usually remedy that by having that child feel important when I assign him tasks to do.

There will always be that one who just won't sit still or has a short attention span. Have him pass out the drinks, help set the table, help set up a game or bring the presents to where you will open them. According to the age assign a task that he is capable of. If you keep an overactive child busy, he is less likely to get bored or into trouble.

But you also need to let the children know that it is YOU who is running the show. In short, don't put up with any troublemakers. Set them straight from the first moment that they get out of line. You can do this without being rude or mean, but set them straight immediately.

You may have a shy child attend. That's fine! If he wants to sit out a game and just watch, let him. He may be a little afraid of trying some games, or he just may not be social. Don't pressure this child. Some may start out timid and come around later. If you don't make them feel uncomfortable by making a scene about it, they may feel more comfortable with you.

A child may even want to sit out a game if it is too hot outside and you are playing active games. By all means, let that child sit out the game. Make sure he gets plenty of water if he is too

hot. Some children have a lower heat tolerance than others. Get him in the shade to cool off. If necessary, hand the children wet cool paper towels to cool off.

Although it is a rare occurrence, sometimes a guest will show up with a friend. This has happened to me twice to date. It kind of shocks you when you open the door and in front of you stands this complete stranger. Plan on having a little extra food and favors just in case this should happen to you.

One time a mom called the morning of the party and really put me on the spot by asking if her babysitter's child could come (who, by the way, was a wild child that my daughter didn't care for). It was a rainy day and we had planned for an outdoor party, which meant that my house was already really going to be cramped. We had only planned for a certain amount of guests and I had to tell her no. I really felt bad, but I couldn't have any of my guests that were invited do without.

Somehow, the child still ended up working her way into the party later in the day. There really wasn't much that we could do, and in order to spare her feelings we asked her to join us. Basically, when this type of situation happens, you just sort of have to play it by ear.

▲ PARTY FAVORS ▲

It is best to wait until it is time for guests to go home before handing out the goody bags; otherwise the children will get them mixed with one another's. To help prevent this, label each child's bag with his name. You can use a variety of things for favor holders. For example:

- Use paper bags and decorate with stencils, sponge paint or stickers. Fold over the top of the bag, and punch two holes at the top with a hole puncher. Thread a ribbon through the holes, and tie the ribbon in a bow. Curl the ends of the ribbon. If you like, tie a nametag or a toy onto the ribbon.
- Use beach pails for spring and summer parties.
- Allow children to make their own goody bags as they arrive. Supply a paper bag, precut shapes from construction paper, glue, crayons, markers, etc.
- A very pretty way to make a favor holder is to lay all of the favors on top of two different colored sheets of tissue paper. Turn the top sheet of tissue paper so that its 4 corners hang over the lower sheet edges. Bring up all of the corners, and tie with curled ribbon at the middle. If desired, make nametags out of paper and punch each with a hole puncher. Slip the ribbon through the hole before tying.
- Use plastic zippered sandwich bags or miniature beach bags. Paint each child's name on them along with pretty designs.

I like to order my party favors from mail order companies. I get a great discount and don't have to drive all over town trying to find the perfect items to fit the theme. The following are some companies that sell party supplies:

Oriental Trading Co., Inc.
PO Box 3407
Omaha, NE 68103-0407
1-800-228-2269
Website: http://www. oriental. com

U.S. Toy
1227 E. 119th St.
Grandview, MO 64030-1117
1-800-255-6124
(in Kansas City area call 816-761-5900)
Fax: 1-816-761-9295 (24 hours)

Stumps
PO Box 305
South Whitley, IN 46787-0305
1-800-348-5084 (6 days a week)
Fax: 1-219-723-6976 (24 hours)

Rhode Island Novelty
675 West Shore Rd.
Warwick, RI 02889
1-800-528-5599
(in Warwick, RI area call 401-739-6090)
Fax: 1-800-448-1775 (24 hours)

When shopping, keep a sharp eye out for toys on clearance sale. These can be found in many stores throughout the year. It's not necessary to spend a lot of money on favors.

Each theme in this book has many, many great favor ideas, but you couldn't possibly use them all. Pick the ones that you like best. Even some of the craft projects the children do can be considered their take home party favor.

I do think that it is very important to send all children home with something. It's sad when party favors aren't given at a party. The children so look forward to them. Even if all that your budget allows is inexpensive candy, send your guests home with something. Favors are a way of saying "Thank you for coming."

Fill the bags as guests call you and tell you that they will be coming. Set them aside in a box or basket. If possible, fill the bags with items that fit the theme. During the party, keep the goody bags close to where you will be near the end of the party. If it is an indoor party, keep the bags near the front door. If you are having an outdoor party, bring the bags outside at the end of the party.

Whether you give goody bags to your own children is up to you. What I usually do is give any extra bags, usually meant for someone who couldn't come, to my children. You may want to have extras on hand in case you have any uninvited guests, such as the sibling of a guest. It's rare, but could happen.

Some parents give any extra bags or favors that they don't want to siblings of guests when they come to pick up a brother or sister. You may prefer to put them away for your next party.

One fun way to give a take home party favor is to play a game called "Blind Choice." Wrap presents and hang from a clothesline or rope hung between two trees. Blindfold one child at a time and tell them to pick a present. Then cut the package from the line. Make sure presents are suitable for both boys and girls, if necessary, or have two lines, one for boys and one for girls.

⚐ TEACHING ⚐ THANKS

Having your child write thank you notes is good social etiquette. Thank you notes should be sent out within a week of giving the party. I think children 8 and up should be mature enough to handle writing a thank you note. It is also a good idea for them to write one to relatives and friends who live too far away to give a great big thank you hug to. Even if your child is too young to write, he will love drawing a thank you picture. You could have them dictate a note to you, so that you may write it on the picture for them. If they are old enough, have them sign their own name.

Writing all of the notes out at one time can be tiresome. Let them space out the time between writing the notes, if necessary.

Although it is not as personal and does not acknowledge the individual gift given, your child may want to write a generic note to put into each goody bag. This note may read, "Thank you for coming to my party, and thank you for the gift. I'm really glad that you could come!"

I cannot stress this enough: Never, never let a guest go home without being thanked! Even if your child is only two years old, he should say thank you. Every guest should be walked to the door upon leaving, if possible. I know things are usually crazy at the end of the party with many parents showing up all at once, but your child should acknowledge that the guest is leaving.

Your child should politely say, "Thank you for coming to my party, and thank you for the gift. I'm really glad that you could come!" This shows appreciation and lets the guests go home feeling good.

It is also a good idea to teach your child to thank a host when attending a birthday party. When you're on the way to a party, create a scenario in which your child thanks the host for inviting him to the party. By setting up the situation for your child, you'll prepare him to use good manners that will stick with him for a lifetime.

☝ FAMILY ☝ TRADITIONS

In all the hustle-bustle of planning the party, don't forget to set aside time for special family celebrations. Even small remembrances can become cherished traditions over time. Here are a few suggestions to get you started.

Plant a Tree

Plant a tree on your child's first birthday. It will grow right along with your child. Each year take a picture of your child next to the tree to show how they both have grown over the years.

Decorate Your Child's Room

The night before your child's actual birthday, sneak into your child's room after your child is sound asleep, and decorate the room with balloons and crepe paper streamers. Put a banner across the door that reads, "HAPPY BIRTHDAY." Put a box of candy on the dresser. What a great surprise to wake up to a decorated room. What a great way to start a day. Already in a great mood, your child is sure to have a wonderful day!

Doodle Pictures

If you can't be at home when your child wakes up on his birthday, be sure to draw a happy birthday picture. Nothing fancy, just a simple picture will do. Leave the picture on a nightstand, dresser or a placemat on the kitchen table. It should make your child's day — even if he can't give you a giant squeezy hug until after you get home from work.

Birthday Muffins

On the morning of your child's actual birthday, serve him a muffin for breakfast with a lit candle in it. You could bake the muffin with a piece of chocolate in it for an added surprise.

Money, Money, Money

Each year give your child an amount of money corresponding with his age. To add an element of surprise, wrap the money in foil and hide it within one of his meals, perhaps in a birthday muffin. Be sure that the birthday child gets the section of food with the surprise.

Add to a Collection

Start a collection of books, recordings, stamps, coins, dolls, books, etc., and add an item to it each year.

ABC, 123

Bring out your child's old school papers and show him how much his handwriting has changed in a year. Even pictures he has drawn will show a noticeable difference.

Baby Book

Bring out your child's old baby book and go through it with him. Measure his height and record it in the book. Do this a couple of days after the birthday or on your child's actual birthday.

Quiet Picture Time

A couple of days after the party is over, and all is quiet on the homefront, sit down with your child, and go through old photo albums. Reminisce about previous birthday parties.

🎉 PRECAUTIONS 🎉

The following precautions are not meant to scare you. Chances are that you probably already practice most of them, but just in case one or two of them have never crossed your mind, I'll go over them anyway.

- Most people don't think of balloons as unsafe toys, but small children and pets can easily choke on uninflated balloons or pieces of a popped balloon. Remove any deflated or popped pieces immediately. Do not take metallic balloons outdoors. If they come in contact with power lines they can cause serious problems.

- Keep some bandages on hand, just in case.

- Never leave handguns or fireworks where children can get at them. Keep them locked up.

- Learn some basic CPR — not only for a party, but also for your own family.

- Put any medications or chemicals in a locked cabinet.

- Don't leave any party guests unattended, especially near water.

- Put pets away in a safe place. Make sure that they are comfortable and well fed.

- When purchasing party favors for children under three the parts should not be smaller than 1¼".

- Scour your yard for hazards. Put away hammocks, clear the yard of any debris, check fences and decks for popped nails, check wire fences for any sharp points sticking out.

- Keep all party decorations away from heat sources; they could catch on fire.

- Keep aerosol cans of spray streamers away from fire (including birthday candles). The substance is highly combustible.

I hope that I haven't overwhelmed you with all of this information. Reading it may make you think that birthday parties are harder than they really are. I would imagine that you are wondering, "Wow, is it really worth it?"

My answer is, "You bet it's worth it!" When your child gives you a great big hug after the party, and thanks you for giving him the best day of his life, then you will realize it was all worth it. That alone should be incentive enough to get you excited about planning your child's next birthday party. Happy partying to you!

Parties for Toddlers

A birthday party for a child of 1 or 2 years old should only include the immediate family and very close friends. A large party with too much commotion may be overwhelming for a toddler. Make sure that the party is after naptime and that the birthday child is well rested.

Keep the party simple. Games will not be necessary, nor a lot of decorations, unless you will be having older children who will be expecting them. A few balloons and some crepe paper in the party room should be enough.

Use colorful, disposable tableware for easy cleanup. You may want to skip the tablecloth, since toddlers sometimes pull them off the table.

When it is time for cake and ice cream, make sure that you have the floor protected — it *will* be messy. Give the birthday child a cupcake with a lit candle or two to blow out. Watch that he doesn't burn himself while everyone sings happy birthday to him.

Let him blow out the candle; and then let him attack his cupcake or piece of cake on his own with his hands. Have your camera ready, because he will be quite a sight to see. His hands and face will be covered with cake and icing. It's his big day, so let him enjoy that cake, mess and all. Just be sure to cover his clothing with a bib, or it will never be the same again.

After he is all washed up, move on to opening the presents, *before* he gets tired and cranky. Remember to get plenty of pictures and videotape, especially if this is a first birthday. Give him some time to play with his new toys, as long as there are no siblings or other toddlers who will fight with him over his birthday treasures.

If young nieces, nephews and close friends attend, and the birthday child isn't cranky, play a couple of games. Play some toss games with a large ball, or blow bubbles and see who can catch them. Young elementary school aged children and teenagers love to play with toddlers. They will have a good time whether you plan a game or not.

After the birthday child goes down for his nap, or to sleep for the evening, you might entertain the older children with a few more age appropriate games — that is, if you are up to it.

⚜ FOOD ⚜

Plan the meal ahead of time. Make a meal that can be frozen and defrost it the day before the party. Some choices you may consider are casseroles, gumbos, stews, and lasagna. Or simply cook hot dogs or hamburgers on the grill. Chances are, you won't have a lot of time to cook an elaborate meal.

Consider purchasing a party platter at your grocery store, with deli meats and cheeses. Set some bread rolls out and let everyone help themselves. Serve with chips and pickles.

Here are a couple of cake ideas that work well for toddler parties.

Balloon Cakes

You will need:

1 package of cake mix, plus ingredients as box directs
1 paper cupcake pan liner
3 cups of any color icing you choose
1 cup of another colored icing, optional
Sugar sprinkles, optional
Wrapping paper ribbon

What to do:

1. Grease and flour two 8- or 9-inch round cake pans. Line a muffin pan cup with one paper cupcake liner. (You will be baking two round cake layers and one cupcake.)

2. Preheat oven and prepare cake mix as directed on package.

3. Pour a small amount of batter in the one cupcake pan liner. Pour the remaining batter into the round pans, dividing batter equally.

4. Bake cupcake 20 minutes and bake cake 30 minutes or until a cake tester inserted into a center comes out clean.

5. Cool cakes and cupcake in pans on wire racks 10 minutes. Remove from pans and cool completely on wire racks.

6. Remove the paper liner from the cupcake and cut it in half.

7. Freeze the cupcake and cake layers uncovered, for about an hour to make frosting easier.

8. Remove from freezer and arrange, as shown in diagram (fig. 1a & b), on a foil-covered board. Place the cupcake halves next to the round cakes to appear as the knot of the balloon.

9. Frost the cakes. If desired, add large polka dots on top of one and write a birthday message on the other using a different color frosting.

10. To each cake, just before serving, add a bow with a strand of ribbon dangling from it to appear as a balloon string. This is purely for decoration. As soon as the cakes are presented, quickly remove the ribbons and discard.

(a)   (b)

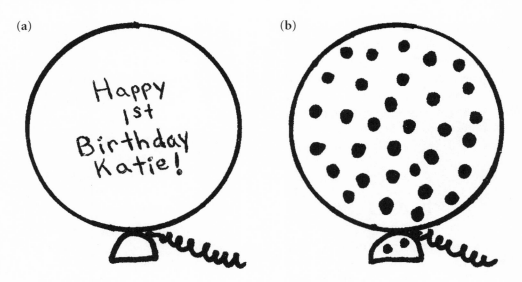

Fig. 1. Balloon Cakes

Variation: If you will be making these cakes for an older child, use candies such as sliced gumdrops for the polka dots.

Party Hat Cake

You will need:

One box of cake mix, plus ingredients as box directs
One paper cupcake pan liner
Yellow frosting, about 3 cups
Blue frosting, about 1 cup

What to do:

1. Grease and flour a 9 × 13 inch cake pan and line a muffin pan cup with one paper cupcake liner. (You will be baking a sheet cake and one cupcake.)

2. Preheat oven and prepare cake mix as directed on package.

3. Pour a small amount of batter in the one cupcake pan liner.

Pour the remaining batter into the 9 × 13 inch cake pan.

4. Bake cupcake 20 minutes and bake sheet cake 30 minutes or until cake tester inserted in center comes out clean.

5. Cool sheet cake and cupcake in pans on wire racks 10 minutes. Remove from pans and cool completely on wire racks.

6. Remove paper liner from cupcake. Cut the sheet cake into a triangle shape, as shown in diagram on next page (fig. 2a).

7. Freeze cake and cupcake uncovered for about an hour to make frosting easier.

8. Place the cut triangle cake on a foil-covered board, and frost yellow.

9. Frost the cupcake blue and set at the tip of the triangle.

10. Frost a blue ruffled border along the hat bottom and frost blue polka dots on the hat.

Variation: If you will be making this cake for an older child, use candies such as M & M's or sliced gumdrops for the polka dots.

(a)

(b)

Fig. 2. Party Hat Cake

Teddy Bear
Tea Party

This is a great party for preschoolers who are a little unsure about going to their first birthday party. Having an old pal (their favorite teddy bear) to hug or have close by may help children feel more at ease. Just in case anyone forgets to bring a teddy bear, have a couple of extras on hand for guests to borrow.

🎉 BEAR 🎉
INVITATION

You will need:

Light brown construction paper or cardboard

Scissors

Glue

Small wiggle eyes (found at craft stores), optional

Black markers

What to do:

1. Cut out teddy bear shapes as shown in illustration (fig. 3a & b).

2. Write invitation on one side.

3. Glue wiggle eyes onto other side, or draw on eyes.

4. Draw on a mouth, a muzzle and a heart shaped nose.

🎉 DECORATIONS 🎉

- Decorate the mailbox with bright primary colored balloons and crepe paper steamers.

- Make paw prints out of brown paper bags or brown construction paper, and place them on the sidewalk to the front door. On each one write, "Hello" or "Welcome" to each of the guests. Stick the paw prints to your

(a)

(b)

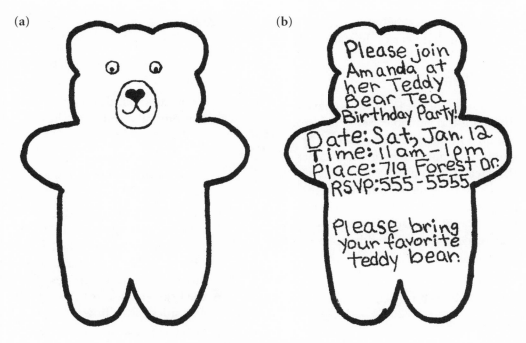

Please join Amanda at her Teddy Bear Tea Birthday Party!
Date: Sat., Jan. 12
Time: 11 am – 1 pm
Place: 719 Forest Dr.
RSVP: 555-5555

Please bring your favorite teddy bear.

Fig. 3. Bear Invitation

sidewalk by putting a few loops of masking tape on the backside of each one. Face them so that your guests can read them as they walk up the sidewalk.

- Decorate the front door or gate with a bear that is made out of light brown paper or cardboard.

- Use a pretty tablecloth for the table. For tableware use fancy teacups, saucers and nice napkins.

- Set a small bear in the center of the table, or a pretty flower arrangement. Give flowers away as party favors.

- Tie a helium filled balloon to each bear's arm as guests arrive.

- Songs to play: "Me and My Teddy Bear," "The Teddy Bears' Picnic," "(Let Me Be Your) Teddy Bear" (Elvis Presley), "Party Teddy Bears" (Rosenshontz), "Teddy Bear" (John

McCutcheon) and "Teddy Bear Hug" (Raffi).

🎉 FOOD 🎉

Bear Sandwiches

Use a bear-shaped cookie cutter to cut bread into bear shapes. Spread one bread bear with peanut butter. Spread the other with a berry-type jelly or honey. Serve with fish-shaped crackers.

Beary Good Fruit Salad

Bears are berry lovers, but so are kids. Put raspberries, blueberries, strawberries and grapes in small individual custard cups or small clear disposable drinking cups for each guest. Let the children pretend to feed the berries to their teddy bears. Just remind them that berries do stain cloth.

Bear Tea

Use a fancy teapot, if you have one that's not too valuable. Serve tea (not too hot) in fancy teacups. Allow the children to put honey or sugar cubes in their tea. Try to purchase honey in a plastic bear-shaped container. If the children don't like tea, put apple juice in the teapot instead. Give them empty play teacups for their teddy bears to sip from.

Teddy Bear Cake

You will need:

1 box of cake mix, plus ingredients as box directs

1 can or 2 cups chocolate frosting

1 can or 2 cups pink frosting

2 round, 1½ inch, chocolate peppermint patties

1 marshmallow

Several small round candies, such as M & M's

Red string licorice

What to do:

1. Prepare and bake cake in two 8- or 9-inch round cake pans as directed.

2. Cool cake rounds completely. Cut one cake round as shown in diagram (fig. 4a).

3. Assemble cake on a foil-covered board as shown in diagram (fig. 4b).

4. Put pink frosting in a decorator's bag. Using a star tip, frost a pink circle to form the bear's muzzle. Make two smaller half circles to form the insides of the bear's ears. Frost the top and sides of the bow.

5. Using the star tip and chocolate icing, frost the rest of the bear.

6. Cut the ends off the marshmallow, and place on the bear for eyes. Use candies for the pupils and attach with a dab of icing.

7. Put one chocolate mint at the top of the pink circle for the nose, and one into the center of the bow.

8. Cut licorice into two pieces, and place under the nose on the

(a)

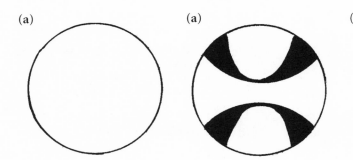

(b)

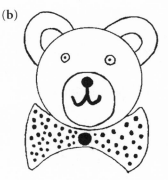

Fig. 4. Teddy Bear Cake

pink frosting to form the mouth. Place candies onto the bow to make polka dots.

🎉 BEAR 🎉 INTRODUCTIONS

After everyone has arrived, seat children in a circle and let them tell their bears' names. If they like, let them tell something else about their bears. They might want to tell how long they have had their bears, if they sleep with their bears every night, who gave them their bears, etc.

🎉 CRAFTS 🎉

Paper Plate Hats

You will need:

One paper plate for each guest
Scissors
Crepe paper
Curled ribbon
Artificial flowers
Glue

What to do:

1. Before the party, cut a slit about 1 inch in from the edge of each plate on each side. Make the slit wide enough to slip the crepe paper through.
2. Slip the crepe paper through on both sides. Make crepe paper long enough to tie a bow under the child's chin.
3. During the party, let the children decorate their hats with ribbons and artificial flowers.

Variation: Purchase inexpensive straw hats and decorate them instead of the paper plates.

Bear Placemats

You will need:

12 × 18 inch sheets of brown paper, one sheet per guest
Scissors
Crayons or markers
Wiggle eyes, optional
Glue, optional

What to do:

1. Before the party, cut one bear shape out of each sheet of paper, the size of a placemat.
2. As children arrive have them draw faces on the bear shapes. Have a sample bear placemat done, to give them an idea of how a bear's face should look.
3. If desired, let them glue wiggle eyes on the faces.

🎉 GAMES AND 🎉 ACTIVITIES

Bear Contest

You will need:

Yellow and blue construction paper
Scissors that cut zigzag

Glue

Tape

What to do:

1. Before the party, cut circles out of the yellow paper with the zigzag scissors.

2. Cut ribbons out of the blue paper.

3. Glue the circles to the tops of the ribbons.

4. During the party, hold a bear contest and write on each ribbon the award given. Some examples are: smallest, biggest, cutest, happiest, fuzziest, most colorful, oldest, newest, most decorated, most cuddly, etc. Let the children help judge. Tape the ribbon to each bear as it gets its award.

Teddy Bear, Teddy Bear

This is a chant that is traditionally used while jumping rope. If your guests aren't skilled at jumping rope alone, two adults may hold the rope, one at each end. The adults turn the rope, while one child at a time takes a turn at jumping to the beat of the chant. If they are still too young for that, just do this as an activity, moving as the following words describe.

Teddy Bear, Teddy Bear,
Turn around,
Teddy Bear, Teddy Bear,
Touch the ground,
Teddy Bear, Teddy Bear,
Show your shoe,
Teddy Bear, Teddy Bear,
That will do!

Teddy Bear, Teddy Bear,
Go upstairs [pretend to step],
Teddy Bear, Teddy Bear,
Say your prayers,
Teddy Bear, Teddy Bear,
Switch off the light,
Teddy Bear, Teddy Bear,
Say goodnight.

Stung by the Bee

This is a version of the old favorite, "Hot Potato."

You will need:

Stuffed bee or a cardboard decorated bee

Music

Lollipops, optional

What to do:

1. Seat all children in a circle. Hand the bee to the birthday child.

2. At the start of the music, the birthday child passes the bee to the child on his left. The children keep passing the bee clockwise until the music stops.

3. When the music stops, the child stuck with the bee is out of the game. To avoid any hurt feelings give each child a lollipop as he goes out, or send him to the Bear's Den for a goody (see the following activity). This is especially important with children of preschool age.

4. The game continues until there are two children left. The one who does not get stuck with the bee wins a prize.

The Bear's Den

As guests are out of the game "Stung by the Bee," send them to this special cave for a re-"treat." Cover a card table with a blanket, leaving one end open. Secure blanket with clothespins. Hide one piece of candy inside for each guest.

Seek the Beehive

You will need:

A yellow or brown balloon

A small prize, or even a prize for each child (e.g., rings, candy, stickers)

String

What to do:

1. Before the party, place one or more small objects into the balloon. Inflate it, and tie it closed. This is the "Beehive."

2. Hang the "Beehive" in a hidden place, either outside from a tree, or somewhere in your home.

3. During the party, tell the children that their bears are hungry for some honey, and that there is a beehive hidden that they must search for. When a child finds the beehive, he wins, or the whole group wins a prize inside of the balloon. Pop the balloon and hand over the prize or prizes. Let them pretend to feed their bears the found honey, while you discard the balloon pieces.

Don't Disturb the Bear

1. Choose one child to be the bear. Have him pretend that he is sleeping, by closing his eyes and lying down like a bear. Make sure that he does not peek.

2. An adult picks a child to go tap the bear and then return back to where he was sitting.

3. When he is seated, all of the children sing (to the tune of "The Farmer in the Dell"): "Don't disturb the bear, don't disturb the bear. Don't you dare go in there. Don't disturb the bear."

4. This is the bear's cue to awaken and stand up. He gets three guesses to figure out who tapped him. If he guesses right, he gets to be the bear again. If he guesses wrong, then whoever tapped him gets to be the bear. The game continues until everyone has had a turn to be the bear. To make sure that everyone has had a turn make a list of names and check them off. This is important to a preschool aged child.

Beehive Piñata

See the chapter on piñatas (end of book).

🎉 FAVOR AND 🎉 PRIZE IDEAS

For a goody holder use a yellow bucket and tape a piece of paper to it that reads, "HONEY," or use a yellow bag and put a bear picture on it, like the one illustrated for the invitation.

Ideas: bear shaped candies or fruit snacks, bear shaped cookies, small stuffed teddy bears, bear stickers, miniature doll tea sets, small storybooks about bears such as "Winnie the Pooh" or "Goldilocks and the Three Bears," flowers, Paper Plate Hats (see craft), balloons stuffed with bee erasers (for older children) and honey-flavored candies such as Bit-O-Honey.

Jack and the Beanstalk Party

No matter how old I become, something about the story "Jack and the Beanstalk" still excites me. It's a classic and will probably always excite children's imaginations. It's a great theme for a party because the possibilities are endless. Read on for a party sky-high with fun!

🎉 BEANSTALK 🎉 INVITATION

Make the invitation as shown in the diagram (fig. 5) using green construction paper. Place the invitation in an envelope with three red beans. It may be necessary to use a 4⅜ × 5¾ inch envelope. Hand-deliver to each guest's home.

Fig. 5. Beanstalk Invitation

🎉 DECORATIONS 🎉

- Hang green and yellow balloons and crepe paper from the mailbox, on the front porch and in the party area.

- Put a sign next to the sidewalk that reads, "Fee, fi, fo, fum, glad to see you chum!"

41

- Put a sign on the front door or on a fence gate that reads, "Shhh! The giant is sleeping. Don't wake him!"
- Put pictures of red beans, cows, beanstalks, a giant, gold, hens, a magic harp or even the hatchet around the house. Make them out of construction paper.
- Play harp music as guests arrive (check your local library, music or department store). You could even play a recording of the story.
- Use a green tablecloth with yellow plates, cups and napkins.
- For a centerpiece, use a stuffed hen, spray-paint plastic Easter eggs gold (regular plastic decorating eggs can be found in craft stores during the off season) and set in a basket, or throw gold plastic coins on the table.

🎉 FOOD 🎉

- Roasted chicken or hen
- Beans — magic ones that make you grow tall (who'll know!)
- Deviled eggs — from the giant's hen
- Applesauce
- Milk — from Jack's cow

Magic Hen Cake

During the party, tell the children to be careful when eating their cake, because there is a hidden gold foil-wrapped chocolate egg or jellybean inside of the cake. Tell them not to swallow it, because whoever finds it wins a prize. (This is for older children.)

You will need:

One box of cake mix, plus ingredients as box directs

White icing, 2 cans or 4 cups

Orange food coloring

One chocolate chip or small round piece of candy

A gold foil-wrapped chocolate egg or jellybean

What to do:

1. Using two 8 or 9 inch round pans, bake and cool the cake as directed, then cut as diagram shows (fig. 6a).
2. Freeze, uncovered, for about an hour to make frosting easier.
3. Assemble as shown in diagram (fig. 6b).
4. Slice a slit anywhere on the cake, and hide the chocolate egg or jellybean in it.
5. Frost the hen body and wing white, reserving some frosting for the beak and foot.
6. Tint the remaining frosting orange, and frost the beak and foot with it.
7. Place the chocolate chip (point side down) or the candy on the head for an eye.

🎉 ARRIVAL 🎉 OF GUESTS

At the beginning of the party you may want to read the story of "Jack and the Beanstalk" (a short story) to get

(a)

(b)

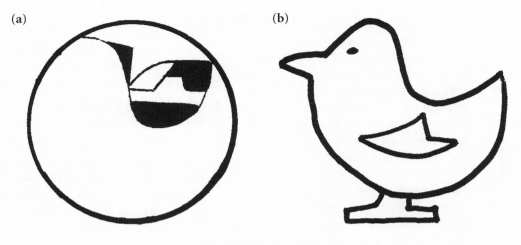

Fig. 6. Magic Hen Cake

everyone in the spirit of the party. If you don't have the story, check with your local library or bookstore.

🎉 CRAFT 🎉

Planting Magic Beanstalks

This activity is sure to mystify your guests!

You will need:

Pre-grown bean plants (see note) in foam cups

Empty foam cups (identical to those containing bean plants), one for each child

Masking tape and a pen

A bucket of potting soil

Small garden shovel

Bean seeds, approximately 3 per child (the ones the guests were instructed to bring, plus a few extra)

Foam cups (just like the others) filled with pre-grown bean plants

What to do:

1. Before the party, label 1 bean plant cup and 1 empty cup with each child's name. Write the name on the masking tape as a label. Hide the bean plant cups in a location inaccessible to the children.

2. During the party, after reading "Jack and the Beanstalk," pass out the empty cups and let the children scoop some potting soil from the bucket into their cups. If possible, do this outside, or in a garage.

3. Once they have all filled their cups with soil, hand each child three "magic" beans to plant in their cups of soil. Let them use their own beans that they brought, if they like.

4. Put these cups of planted "magic" beans in a secret place, such as a locked garage. While you continue with the party, have an adult switch the newly planted bean seed cups with the already grown bean plants.

Make sure that the children do not see the switch and are unaware of anything going on. At the end of the party, when you take the children to get their cups, act surprised that the beans have grown so fast. Say how surprised you are and that they must really be magic beans. How else could they have grown so fast! The children will be amazed. As the children take them home, remind them to water their "beanstalks" when they get home and to be very careful taking them home. You may want to put them in a bag or box at this point. You don't want anyone spilling them in the car on the way home.

Note: If you are unable to purchase bean plants at a store or nursery because they are out of season, plant your own two weeks before the party. Keep them indoors if there is a possibility of frost. If you don't want to risk having your own child see them, ask a friend or relative if you may keep them at their house.

🎉 GAMES AND 🎉 ACTIVITIES

Guess the Number of Beans

You will need:

A small jar
A bag of dried beans, such as red kidney beans
Pencil and paper for each child

What to do:

1. Before the party, fill the jar with the beans, counting them as you put them into the jar.

2. Write down the total, and tape the number underneath the jar.

3. During the party, have each child write down his guess at how many beans are in the jar. Children who are too young to write may just say what they guess. Award a bag of jellybeans to the one who guesses the closest.

Beanbag Toss

You will need:

Beanbags or plastic zippered snack bags filled with small dried beans
Chalk

What to do:

1. Before the party, make a 9-square grid within one larger square, on the pavement with chalk. On the center square write "sack of gold" or "golden egg." Inside the outer squares write words from the story "Jack and the Beanstalk" such as: bean, magic hen, giant, Jack, cow, vine, harp and hatchet.

2. Line children up and allow them to take turns tossing the beanbag from 6 or 8 feet away onto the pavement. Anyone landing on the center square wins. Either a sack of gold coins (plastic or chocolate) or a golden egg filled with candy would make an appropriate prize. A large plastic Easter egg

spray-painted gold makes for a great golden egg. Perhaps you have one stored away from last Easter that you can use.

Hunt for the Giant's Gold

You will need:

Chocolate gold foil-covered coins or gold plastic coins (use plastic if it is warm outside)

Cellophane or plastic sandwich bags

Wrapping paper ribbon

Paper bags to carry gold, optional

What to do:

1. Before the party, write the children's names on the paper bags, if using them.
2. Place a few coins into individual plastic sandwich bags or onto the center of cut squares of cellophane, and tie with ribbon.
3. The day of the party, hide the sacks of gold. Hand each child a paper sack to hold their gold. All race to find it at the signal to go.

Magic Hen Relay

You will need:

Two stuffed animals that resemble a hen or chicken, or two hens cut out of red posterboard and decorated

What to do:

1. Divide children into two equal teams, and line them up behind a start line. Set a goal 20–30 feet away from the start.
2. Hand the first child in each team a hen.
3. At the signal, they are to run with the hen to the goal, pretend to climb down a beanstalk with the hen, then run back to their team and pass the hen to the next teammate in line.
4. The next player then does the same as the first, and the game continues in this manner. The first team to have all of their players finish first wins.

Jack and the Beanstalk Charades

Write the following acts on separate slips of paper:

1. Jack selling the cow in exchange for the beans.
2. Jack throwing the beans out the window and the beanstalk growing.
3. Jack climbing the beanstalk.
4. The giant counting his gold pieces.
5. The hen laying a golden egg.
6. The giant playing the magic harp.
7. Jack chopping down the beanstalk.

What to do:

1. Divide the children into two groups.
2. Choose one child from each team to come stand in front of the others, and have one of

these two children pick a card with a charade written on it. Now both children must act out the charade. They must not say what the charade is out loud or ever talk. They must act out the part.

3. The first team to guess the charade scores a point, and then two other children get chosen to come up. Choose a different set of children at each round, making sure everyone gets a turn to do a charade. When a charade has already been chosen, set it aside. The team who scores the most points wins.

Note: For parties with very young children, an adult must first read the story "Jack and the Beanstalk." Most likely, the adult will have to act out the charades, so that the children can guess.

Bottle Fill

You will need:

One small-necked bottle for each guest

Plenty of small dried beans such as lentils

Two foam or plastic bowls per guest

One spoon per guest

What to do:

1. Give each child a bottle placed in an empty bowl, another bowl full of dried beans, and a spoon.

2. At the signal, they must try to fill their bottles with the beans. The first one to completely fill his bottle wins. They may take

these bottles of beans home with them, or you might consider putting them in a pretty vase for a kitchen decoration after the party.

Know Your Beans

You will need:

Many different types of dried beans

Paper plates

Pencil and paper for each guest

What to do:

1. Put a small amount of each type of bean on separate paper plates. Give each kind of bean a number and write it on the plates.

2. Give each child a pencil and paper, and ask them to write down as many beans as they know or can guess. The one guessing the most correct wins. An appropriate prize might be a packet of bean seeds.

Cup Stacking Contest

You will need:

Green cups

Green construction paper

Glue

Stopwatch or watch secondhand

What to do

1. Before the party, cut leaf shapes out of construction paper and glue them onto the cups.

2. Have children take turns to see who can build the tallest

"beanstalk" by stacking the cups as illustrated (fig. 7). The one to get the most cups to stay up within 30 seconds wins. An appropriate prize would be a packet of seeds or jellybeans.

Fig. 7. Cup Stacking Contest

Bean Bingo

Play regular bingo from store-bought bingo cards. Give the children bean seeds for markers.

Bean Tic-Tac-Toe

This game is a twist on the old time version of drawing X's and O's.

You will need:

Paper and pen

Two bags of different colored beans

What to do:

1. Before the party, draw a 9-square grid for the "game-board" on a sheet of paper. Make one game-board for every two guests.

2. During the party, ask children to choose a partner. Hand one player about 4 beans of one color, and hand the other player 4 beans of another color. Have some extras on hand (they may lose some).

3. The object of the game is to get a straight line or a row of 3 in your own color. The rows may be either vertical, horizontal or diagonal. Each player takes one turn at a time placing one of his beans on the board until someone wins or the board is covered. If no one wins, that is called "cats," and the board is cleared and played again until someone wins. If you want to make this more of a challenge, have the players keep score. The first child on each team to score ten points wins.

Game to Buy

Purchase the game "Don't Spill the Beans" by Milton Bradley, sold at most toy stores, and play it.

🎉 FAVOR AND 🎉 PRIZE IDEAS

Sacks of jellybeans, gold foil-covered chocolate coins or eggs, gold-painted plastic Easter eggs filled with goodies, bean seed packets, bean plants (see craft), small stuffed hens, small books of the story "Jack and the Beanstalk," toy hatchets, plastic gold coins, growth charts, bottles of colorful beans (see game Bottle Fill).

Camelot Party

Does your child like to hear medieval tales about kings, queens, dragons, or knights in shining armor? What child doesn't? Maybe your child is fascinated by Merlin's magic. Whip up this party and create some magic of your own! With just a wave of your magic wand you can turn your home into an enchanted castle. As the old saying goes, one's home is one's castle, and at this castle kids rule!

For a good mood-setter for your family, one or two nights before the party rent the movie *The Sword in the Stone* or *King Arthur and the Knights of the Round Table*.

🎉 SCROLL 🎉 INVITATION

Use tan colored parchment paper or computer paper that looks like a scroll (found in most office supply stores). Write in archaic-looking penmanship or use your

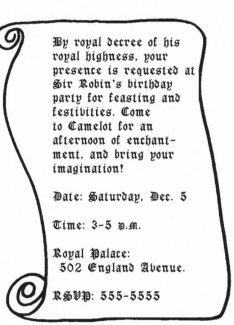

By royal decree of his royal highness, your presence is requested at Sir Robin's birthday party for feasting and festivities. Come to Camelot for an afternoon of enchantment, and bring your imagination!

Date: Saturday, Dec. 5

Time: 3–5 P.M.

Royal Palace:
502 England Avenue.

RSVP: 555-5555

Fig. 8. Scroll Invitation

computer to do the job. See illustration (fig. 8).

🎩 DECORATIONS 🎩

- Hang balloons and crepe paper from the mailbox, on the front porch and in the party area. For a boy's party use red, yellow and black. For a girl's party, use pastel colors such as purple, pink, and yellow.

- Put a sign on the front door that reads, "Welcome to Camelot."

- Make shields from construction paper with emblems on them as illustrated (fig. 9).

- Hang foil-covered cardboard swords on the wall in a criss-cross fashion.

Fig. 9. Shield Emblems

- Hang pictures of Merlin the Magician, owls, a sword stuck in a stone, magic wands, knights, kings, queens, unicorns, etc.

- Use a round table to eat at, if possible.

- Put a toy castle on the table for a centerpiece, or make one out of cereal boxes, oatmeal containers, toilet paper tubes, paper towel tubes, cans, etc. Decorate the "towers" and "walls" with construction paper. Make cone roofs out of paper for each tower. Glue small flags to toothpicks and push into the top of each cone. Cut

Fig. 10. Castle

out a drawbridge and attach string to it. Leave it slightly open for added effect. See illustration (fig. 10).

- Cover a large book such as an old encyclopedia with a cover that reads, "Magic Spells," and put it on your coffee table for the activity Magic Spells.

- Suspend stars and crescent-moon shapes from the ceiling with fishing line. Make the shapes out of cardboard and cover with aluminum foil.

- Play songs like, "Puff the Magic Dragon" (Peter, Paul and Mary), "The Unicorn Song" (The Irish Rovers), or play medieval, Renaissance or Celtic music. One recording that you can buy is an album from the Medieval Times Dinner Theater called "Medieval Times Dinner Original Theme Songs." This can be purchased in their gift shops or ordered over the phone. At this time they have dinner theaters in the following areas: Lyndhurst NJ; Dallas TX; Buena Park CA; Kissimmee FL; and Toronto, Ontario. They have retail stores in New York at Times Square and Schaumburg IL. For more information call 1-800-436-4386.

☂ FOOD ☂

- Chicken drumsticks, preferably roasted or barbecued
- Cheese squares
- Grapes
- Bread rolls
- Grape juice, preferably served in goblets

-or-

- Merlin's Magic Punch: Make a lime punch. Float a blue plastic plate in the punch, with a matching blue cone on top that is made of construction paper. Decorate the cone part by gluing on yellow stars and moon crescents made of construction paper.

Off with His Head!

Serve gingerbread men. See who can eat their cookie the quickest.

Merlin's Wizard Hat Ice Creams

You will need:

- Sugar cones, one per child
- Paper cupcake liners (or blue plastic plates, if you have a large freezer)
- Blue frosting, optional
- Yellow frosting

What to do:

1. Fill the sugar cones with ice cream; work quickly so that ice cream won't melt.
2. Set each cone on top of a paper cupcake liner or blue plate and freeze.
3. Taking only one cone out of the freezer at a time, frost the entire cone with blue frosting.
4. Pipe on yellow stars with yellow frosting and a star tip.
5. Place back in the freezer. Cover when frosting becomes frozen. Take out when needed.

Queen of Hearts Cupcakes

You will need:

A box of cake mix, plus ingredients as box directs

Paper cupcake pan liners

Aluminum foil

One 16-oz. can or 2 cups of pink icing

½ cup white icing, optional

What to do:

1. Line a muffin pan with paper cupcake liners. Place a small rolled ball of foil between each liner and the pan, pressing in toward the center so the paper is indented into a shape of a heart.
2. Prepare cake mix as directed, and pour into paper cups. Bake and cool as directed.
3. Frost the cupcakes pink.
4. If desired, outline the hearts with white frosting, using a

frosting bag and a small star tip.

Sword in the Stone Cupcakes

Bake a batch of cupcakes and frost them gray. Stick a sword shaped toothpick into the top of each.

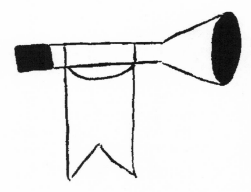

Fig. 11. Trumpet

♟ ARRIVAL ♟ OF GUESTS

Honorable Introductions

As each guest arrives, the court herald (a parent or teen) announces the arrival of each guest by blowing a toy trumpet or a real trumpet. If neither is available, the court herald can pretend by making a trumpet sound. If desired, make the trumpet look authentic by hanging a felt or cloth banner from it with string as illustrated (fig. 11). The court herald says, "Let me introduce our noble guest _____," and announces each guest with an honorary title such as; "Sir Bobby, Knight of the Realm (Kingdom)," "Lady Elizabeth of King Street," "Maiden Emily of Orchard Road," "Prince John of His Family's Palace," etc.

Story Time

If you can find a shortened children's version of the story "King Arthur and the Knights of the Round Table" or "The Sword and the Stone," read it to the children. You may want to read it them shortly after everyone

has arrived. This will help the children who are unfamiliar with the story understand all of the games and the meanings behind them. This isn't necessary for everyone to have a good time, but it would be nice.

♟ CRAFTS ♟

Merlin's Magic Wands

The boys can use these as Merlin the Magician wands, and the girls can use them as fairy princess wands.

You will need:

A star shape for tracing (e.g., cookie cutter, toy sheriff's badge or stencil)

Drinking straws or wooden dowels, one per guest

Colored posterboard

Two or three different colors of curling ribbon or cloth ribbon

Tape

Clear drying glue

Paintbrushes

Glitter

Shirt box, optional

Newspaper, to protect table

What to do:

1. Before the party, trace the star shapes onto the colored poster-board and cut them out.

2. As guests arrive, let them spread glue onto their stars with a paintbrush and pour glitter onto the glue. Warning: This is very messy. A way to keep your house clean is to put the stars in a shirt box and then pour the glitter over them. Shake off the excess glitter into the box.

3. Tape stars to straws or dowels.

4. Tie ribbon onto straws or dowels. If using curling ribbon, curl with a pair of scissors. If using cloth ribbon tie into a bow for the girls. Boys may choose not to have any ribbon. Let them decide.

Merlin Hats

You will need:

Blue construction paper, 18 × 24 inches, one sheet per child

Tape

Yellow construction paper

Scissors

Star shaped stencil or cookie cutter

Moon shaped stencil or cookie cutter

Glue

Hole puncher

12-inch pieces of string, 2 per child

Newspaper, to protect table

What to do:

1. Before the party, trace the star and moon shapes onto the yellow construction paper.

2. During the party, take each sheet of blue paper and roll it into a cone shape for a hat. Cut away the excess paper from the rim, creating a perfect cone shape, circular at the rim.

3. Fit each hat to the child who will be wearing it, and tape it accordingly.

4. Let the children cut out the moon and star shapes and glue them onto the hats.

5. Punch one hole into each side of the hat.

6. Thread a piece of string through each hole and knot it at one end so it will stay in place. Tie these strings under the child's chin to keep the hat on.

Princess Hats

You will need:

Pink or purple construction paper, 18 × 24 inches, one sheet per child

Tape

Scissors

Tulle, netting or chiffon, or similar fabric

Hole puncher

12-inch pieces of string, 2 per child

What to do:

1. Before the party, cut the chiffon into 24 × 24 inch squares.

2. During the party, take each sheet of paper and roll it into a

cone shape. Cut away the excess paper from the rim, creating a perfect cone shape, circular at the rim. Stuff one square of the fabric into the tip of each cone, allowing it to trail behind.

3. Fit each hat to the child who will be wearing it, and tape it accordingly.

4. Punch one hole into each side of the hat.

5. Thread a piece of string through each hole and knot it at one end so it will stay in place. Tie these strings under the child's chin to keep the hat on.

Masquerade Dance Mask

Masquerade balls were very popular in England shortly after the Middle Ages. Guests wore elaborate costumes, including masks much like the following craft.

You will need:

Thin wooden dowels, 12 to 18 inches long
White paint
White or pink posterboard
Craft knife
Glue
Tape
Craft feathers
Glitter glue
Craft jewels or sequins
Newspaper, to protect table

What to do:

1. Before the party, paint the dowels white and allow them to dry.

2. Cut the masks out of posterboard as shown in illustration (fig. 12). Use a craft knife to cut the eyeholes.

3. Glue dowels to each mask, then tape to secure.

4. During the party, set all of the craft materials out on a table and let the children decorate the masks any way they like.

5. Play some waltz music or music of the Middle Ages and invite all of the children to dance in your grand ballroom — i.e., your family room or basement.

Fig. 12. Masquerade Dance Mask

🎉 GAMES AND 🎉 ACTIVITIES

Magic Spells

This really is a great activity, and the children are just amazed by the smoking effect of the dry ice. Now that the children have made their magic wands, ask them to help you cast a magic spell!

You will need:

- A small chunk of dry ice (found at a welding shop, or look under "Ice" in the Yellow Pages of the phone directory)
- A bowl (if you can get a black cauldron, such as one from Halloween, that would be great)
- A cup of water

What to do:

1. Before the party, put the chunk of dry ice into the bowl, and put it in a safe place where no one can touch it. It would be a good idea to keep it in a locked area or freezer until needed.

2. During the party, read a pretend magic spell from your book of magic spells (see Decorations).

3. Ask the children to repeat the spell and wave their magic wands over the bowl of dry ice.

4. Next pour some water over the dry ice and watch it smoke. The children will be amazed!

Caution: DO NOT let the children touch the dry ice or get too close to it, since the temperature is 109° below zero and can burn the skin. DO NOT touch it with your bare hands. Use latex rubber gloves or a pair of metal kitchen tongs when handling the ice. Store it in a safe place until needed. It would be a good idea to try and purchase the dry ice the day of the party or the day before the party, since it evaporates quite quickly. Keep it in an airtight container until needed.

Dragon Tales

Seat all of the children in a circle. An adult or the birthday child starts telling a story about a dragon. Go clockwise around the circle, allowing each child a turn to add to the story. Each child may talk for about one minute, or less if he chooses. Go as long as you wish to end the story. You should try to let the birthday child come up with the ending to the story, if possible

Note: Make sure that you videotape this story. You will want to hear it for years to come.

Swords in the Stone

In the various stories of King Arthur there was only one sword stuck in the stone, but in this game you will have many.

You will need:

Several cocktail swords, at least 2 per guest (found near the toothpicks or mixed drink section of your grocery store)

Gold paint, optional

A paint color that is different than the cocktail swords, such as bright orange, optional

Gray spray paint

A piece of foam, to appear like a stone (found in craft stores)

What to do:

1. Before the party, spray-paint the foam with gray spray paint and allow to dry.

2. Paint the swords gold, if desired. Paint the pointed tip of only one sword a different

color, or if using gold paint leave one tip unpainted. Allow to dry.

3. Stick all of the "swords" in the "stone," just enough to cover the tips.

4. During the party, allow each guest one turn to pull out a sword. The child who pulls the one with the different tip wins.

Note: If you like, use this to let children draw when trying to choose who goes first in a game — after the birthday child, of course.

Search for the Holy Grail

If you have not read the story of King Arthur to the children, explain to them that King Arthur and his Knights of the Round Table spent many years searching for the Holy Grail, and that it is a cup thought to have magical powers!

You will need:

A brass goblet, a plastic champagne glass spray-painted gold, or a wooden goblet

What to do:

1. Hide the goblet or glass either indoors or outdoors. If desired, write clues to find it on paper.

2. Divide the children into two or more groups and send them to find the Holy Grail. Maybe its magic will win them a piece of candy or a prize!

Jousting Relay

You will need:

6 boxes: 2 large, 2 medium and 2 small

2 wrapping paper tubes or safe toy swords for lances

A horn (or, for variation, a handkerchief)

What to do:

1. Divide the children into two equal teams. Line them up behind a starting line. Hand the first two children in line a "lance."

2. Stack the boxes into two piles 20–30 feet away from the starting line. Place the large box on the bottom, the medium box in the middle and the small box on top.

3. At the signal (blow of horn), the first two children from each team must gallop like horses to the boxes with their "lances" and knock down the "knights" (the stacks of boxes — one for each team). They then must gallop back to their teams and hand over the lances to the next children in line. (As soon as the boxes are knocked down, two adults or helpers pick them up before the next child comes.)

4. The next child in each line then must gallop and do the same as the first child. This continues until one team finishes. The first team to finish is declared the Noble Knights or the winning team.

Variation: In medieval times the jousting tournament began when a lady of the court dropped her handkerchief onto the arena field. This was the signal to begin. If you like, have a girl or woman do this honor instead of beginning at the sound of the horn.

Dragon Hide and Seek Tag

You will need:

A card table
A blanket
Clothespins

What to do:

1. Before the party, set up a "dragon's cave" by throwing a blanket over a card table. Leave one end open and secure the blanket with clothespins.

2. To play, have one child be "It" or the dragon, and send him into the "cave." He must cover his eyes and count to 30 aloud while everyone finds a good hiding place.

3. Once he reaches 30 he yells, "Roooar! Ready or not, here I come!" He then seeks the other players. The first child he finds, he tags. He then searches for all the other players.

4. Once everyone has been found, the game begins a new round. The first child to have been found becomes the next "dragon." Play as long as time allows, or until everyone has had a chance to be the dragon.

Variation: Use a garage or shed as the dragon's cave. If the party will be held at night, use a flashlight to play flashlight tag. The beam becomes the dragon's "fire."

Card Castles

You will need:

Two or more decks of cards
A timer

What to do:

1. Divide the children into two or more teams, and give each team a deck of cards.

2. On the carpet, in an open area, have each group sit in its own circle. One child evenly distributes the cards among his team members.

3. At a signal to go, set a timer for 5 minutes, and tell the teams to begin making a tower or "castle." The team with the tallest castle when the timer goes off wins.

4. An appropriate prize for each member of the winning team would be a deck of cards.

Note: Do not play this game on a slick surface such as a table. It will cause the cards to fall.

Court Jesters

You will need:

2 balls (have a third one handy just in case they are better than you expect)
A whistle
Pencil and paper
A stopwatch, optional

What to do:

1. The children all take turns at "juggling" balls. At the blow of a whistle, set the stopwatch, and the child begins tossing the balls into the air and tries to catch them. They shouldn't be expected to be very good at this if they are very young.

2. Once a child drops a ball, stop the stopwatch, blow the whistle again to signal the end of his turn.

3. Write down how long each child tossed the balls without dropping them. The one who kept the balls up in the air the longest wins. An appropriate prize would be a ball or a jester's hat.

To the Dungeon with You!

See Wild West Party games and activities: "Round Up." The Corral becomes the Dungeon.

Merlin's Crystal Ball

See Pirate Party games and activities: "Gypsy Fortune Teller." Have an adult dress as Merlin the Magician, if you like. Make a Merlin hat (see Craft). If possible, have him wear a long fake beard and a blue robe.

Don't Fall into the Moat!

See Pirate Party games and activities: "Walk the Plank." Instead of shark or fish toys, use crocodile toys.

Dragon Archery

You will need:

A bow and arrow with a rubber foam or tip

Large paper dragon (draw on a large sheet of paper)

Rope or clothesline from which to hang the dragon

Clothespins

What to do:

1. Hang the dragon from the rope or clothesline with clothespins.

2. Allow each child three shots at the dragon with the bow and arrow. The one with the most hits wins. Pronounce the winner "champion archer of England."

♟ LEAVING ♟ THE PARTY

At the end of the party, knight each child before handing him a goody bag. They must all kneel down on one knee, as an adult must touch both of their shoulders with a sword and say something like, "I dub thee Sir Bobby, Knight of the Realm (Kingdom)," or "I dub thee Maiden Margaret, Princess of Camelot," etc.

☝ FAVOR AND ☝ PRIZE IDEAS

King and queen crowns, Merlin Hats (see Crafts), Princess Hats (see Crafts), Masquerade Dance Mask (see Crafts), jester hats, swords, shields, toy dragons, toy horses, toy unicorns, Magic Wands (see Crafts), magic tricks, playing cards, play jewelry, small storybooks such as *The Sword and the Stone* or *Robin Hood* and Unicorn Twist lollipops (look like unicorn horns).

Wild Jungle Safari Party

Want to put on a party that your child will go bananas over? Don't monkey around, look no further! In this wildly exciting jungle adventure, imaginations will run free. You will transport your child and guests to the deep dark jungles of Africa, or maybe the Amazon Tropical Rain Forest. If your child is fascinated with jungle movies, loves going to the zoo, or was just born to be wild, then this party is for him or her. Rent the movie *The Jungle Book* or watch television shows about African or Amazon wildlife and cultures to help you get in the spirit. Now go ahead, take a walk on the wild side!

LION INVITATION

Now here's an invitation that will make your child feel like the king of the jungle ... especially if you let him help you make them (see fig. 13 a & b). If you know that your child's friends own camouflage clothes, khaki-type clothes or clothes with animals on them, ask them to wear them.

DECORATIONS

- Decorate the mailbox, front porch and party room with green, black, brown and yellow balloons and crepe paper. You may even be able to find balloons with animal prints on them.

- Hang green crepe paper from trees, front porch and party room to resemble vines. If desired, staple green leaves, made out of green construction paper to the streamers. Place them so that guests must walk through them to enter your house.

- Hang paper monkeys from the crepe paper "vines." Tape them to the

60

(a)

(b)

Fig. 13. Lion Invitation

vines as if they are hanging from their arms.

- Make spiraled snakes by cutting circle shapes from colored paper and spiraling the cut to the center of the circle. Hang from the "vines."

- Decorate the party room with pictures of tigers, monkeys, gorillas, elephants, zebras, crocodiles, leopards and parrots made of construction paper, copied from your computer or even from coloring book pages. Try to make animals that are native to the particular jungle or forest of your theme.

- Hang toy plastic snakes from light fixtures (keeping away from heat source) or place on the party table.

- Decorate the table with a green tablecloth. Use yellow plates, cups and napkins, or try to find ones with jungle animals on them.

- Put plastic or stuffed jungle-type animals on the party table and in the party area.

- Bring any exotic plants that you may have from around the house into the party area.

- Put a picture of a lion made of yellow construction paper on the front door. Add a word bubble that reads, "Ring bell for a ROARING good time!"

- Play a recording of jungle animal sounds, or African drum selections near your front door, so that guests will feel like they are entering the jungle. Your local library or music store may have what you need. Some songs to play are; "On Safari" (Ella Jenkins), "There's a Hippo in My Tub" (Joanie Bartels), "Going to the Zoo" (Raffi), "The Gorilla Song" (Raffi), "Here Sits a Monkey" (Raffi), "In an Elephant World" (Tom Chapin)," "Animal Crackers" (Shirley Temple), "Born to Be Wild" (Steppenwolf), "Three Cool Cats" (The Beatles), "Crocodile Rock" (Elton John), "Stray Cat Strut" (Stray Cats), "Monkees Theme" (The

Monkees), "The Lion Sleeps Tonight" (The Tokens), "Hungry Like the Wolf" (Duran Duran), or "Gitarzan" (Ray Stevens). The first seven songs listed are primarily for younger children.

♟ FOOD ♟

- Peanut butter and jelly sandwiches cut in animal shapes. For a zebra, cut with a horse shaped cutter and put black string licorice across the sandwich to look like stripes.
- Bananas
- Animal crackers or animal shaped iced cookies
- Shelled peanuts

Caution: Do not give peanuts to children under 3. They may choke on them.

Snake Cake

Although the green mamba snakes of Africa are extremely dangerous, this one is very harmless and quite sweet.

You will need:

1 baked Bundt cake (you can use a mix; bake and cool as directed on box)

3 cups green frosting

2 chocolate kisses

2 chocolate chips

Black or red shoestring licorice

Red Fruit Roll-Ups

What to do:

1. Cut the cake in half. Cut the edges of the cake to round them a little. Carve a sharp point out of the end of one half for the tail. Cut a rounded head out of the other half for the head. Make sure that you cut the correct ends by placing them as diagram shows (fig. 14a), like an "S" shape.
2. If desired, freeze uncovered for about one hour to make the frosting spread more easily.
3. Place on a foil-covered board, keeping the flat edges together, again in the "S" shape.
4. Frost the entire cake green.
5. Push chocolate kisses into the top of the head, pointed side down, for the eyes.
6. Push the two chocolate chips into the nose tip, for nostrils.
7. Cut a piece of licorice and put it on the face for the mouth.
8. Cut a "Y" shape out of a piece of a fruit roll and stick it onto the mouth for a tongue, pushing into the icing.
9. Add scales by pressing an icing tip, at its wide end, at a slight angle into the icing.

Note: Although a green mamba is only green, you can jazz up your snake by adding colored stripes, dots or triangle shapes. You could even add candy pieces to the cake.

Animal Cupcakes

If time is short, bake and frost cupcakes, then stick small plastic zoo animals on top.

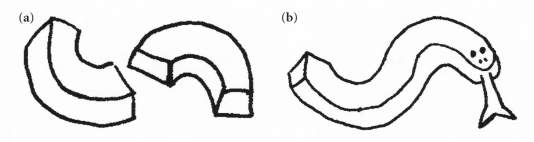

Fig. 14. Snake Cake

🎉 ARRIVAL 🎉 OF GUESTS

It's a Jungle in Here

As guests arrive at the door give them an animal nametag. Use your computer or coloring book pages for some good animal pictures. The picture on the nametag is the animal that the guest must become as he enters the house. When the doorbell rings and the next child comes in, the "lion" must roar like a lion, the "elephant" must trumpet like an elephant, etc. All join in as each guest arrives. Of course the last guest to arrive will also need a turn, so have an adult go around to the door and ring the bell. (The adult must pretend to be surprised when all the animals greet him!)

Note: This game will warm up the children for the game animal charades, if you choose to play it.

🎉 CRAFTS 🎉

Jungle Mural

You will need:

A large sheet of paper (some mail order companies send items wrapped in large sheets of paper; save them!)

Washable paints

One paintbrush per guest

Heavy duty tape such as mailing tape

What to do:

1. Before the party, hang up the paper with the tape. A great place to hang it is on a wooden fence or a brick wall — somewhere that you won't have to worry about paint spills.

2. As guests arrive, hand each a paintbrush and tell them to draw their favorite jungle animal (e.g., lion, tiger, elephant, zebra, snake, monkey, parrot, etc.). An adult may want to join in and paint some foliage.

Scary Tarantulas

The name tarantula was originally given to a wolf spider of Taranto, Italy. In the Middle Ages, it was believed that the poisonous effects of this spider's bite could be eliminated by dancing. This dance became known as the tarantella, hence the name tarantula.

For this craft you will need one adult helper for about every four children, if the children are younger than nine years old.

You will need:

> 4 brown pipe cleaners per guest
> 1 brown 2-inch pom-pom per guest
> Two ¼-inch wiggle eyes per guest
> Glue
> A 2-foot piece of fishing line, one per guest
> 1 popsicle stick or craft stick per child, optional
> A stapler, optional

What to do:

1. Have each child take all four pipe cleaners and twist them around the pom-pom so that they form "legs" under a "spider body."

2. Have them pull the pipe cleaners apart to look like a spider's legs, and bend the tips of each leg out at about 1 inch from the end.

3. Next, tie the fishing line onto the top of the pipe cleaners.

4. Tie the other end of the fishing line to the popsicle stick or craft stick, if using, and staple it in place.

5. Glue the wiggle eyes onto the pom-pom. You now have a tarantula ready to scare unexpecting parents and siblings!

Safari Binoculars

If you've had a child in preschool or elementary school, chances are that you've already seen these once or twice before. They are so simple and kids love them.

You will need:

> 2 toilet paper tubes per guest
> A hole puncher
> Green and black paint, optional
> String
> Scissors

What to do:

1. Before the party, paint the tubes giving them a camouflage look. Allow the paint to dry.

2. At the party, staple each two tubes together.

3. Punch a hole on one side of each tube.

4. Cut a piece of string about 2½ feet long, thread one end through each hole and knot it, making a neck strap.

5. The children can check out the wild things in your yard. Point out birds, squirrels and bugs.

African Drums

I recommend trying this craft before the party, because some balloons are not large enough. But when you find the right size, it makes an excellent drum.

You will need:

Coffee cans with one end removed
(school lunch rooms and restaurants may have good cans for you)

Giant balloons or jumbo balloons

Brown construction paper or brown
paper bags

Scissors

Rubber band or tape

Glue or tape

Markers, crayons or paint

Colored plastic tape or masking tape

File

What to do:

1. Before party, file down any
   sharp edges on the cans. Cut
   the paper to wrap around the
   cans.

2. During the party, let the children decorate the paper with
   markers, crayons or paint.

3. Then let them choose what
   color balloon they would like
   to have on their drum, and cut
   off the neck of the balloon.
   (You could also have the balloons put on the cans before the
   party, if you like.)

4. It may be necessary to have two
   adults put the balloon on the
   can, because it may be a tight
   fit. One may need to stretch the
   balloon over the can, while the
   other helps hold the balloon on
   the can. Tape the balloon to the
   can and secure it with a rubber
   band.

5. Let the child then tape or glue
   their decorated paper to the
   can. Voilà! You now have an
   African drum!

Note: The children may use their
hands to play the drums, or you can
give them sticks wrapped on one end
with a wad of masking tape. Another
idea is to use round lollipops for
drumsticks.

🎉 GAMES AND 🎉 ACTIVITIES

Take a Trip to the Zoo

Take the children to the zoo and
return home afterwards for cake and
ice cream. For children 6 and under it
may be too tiring to do both. Many
zoos have birthday party packages that
include the zoo tour, a meal and a surprise. Some zoos will reserve seats in
their restaurant for your party. You
may even consider using the zoo picnic
area and holding a party there after
touring the zoo. Check to see if your
local zoo has a picnic area. Try not to
plan your party at a zoo during an
event day or near special holidays such
as Mother's Day. The zoo may be
packed with many other people on
those days. You may want to ask the
parents to stay and help you watch
their children.

If you live near a wild animal safari, consider a trip there. Many of
them allow the animals to roam and
graze freely. Some allow you to drive
through the parks with your own vehi-
cle or take a guided bus tour (season-
ally). Many of the animals will come
right up to your window for a scratch
on the head, or a bite to eat. Be sure to
bring plenty of film if you go. If there

is one near your home, check to see if they offer group discounts or party activities. Call well in advance.

Monkey Relay

You will need:

2 bananas

A whistle

What to do:

1. Divide the children into two teams and line them up behind a start line. Mark a goal approximately 20 feet away from the start line. Give a banana to the first child in each line.

2. At the blow of a whistle, the first team member in each line must run, crouched low like a monkey, to the designated goal and back with the banana.

3. They pass the banana to the next team member in line who must do the same. This continues until all of one team's members finish. They are the declared winning team. An appropriate prize would be a banana or banana flavored candy for each team member.

Monkey Shuffle

For some unknown reason this game always has the longest line at our city Kid's Day Festival. Kids just love it. I am assuming that the board represents a cave and the puck a monkey, but no one seems to know.

You will need:

A hockey puck with ball bearings on the bottom

A cardboard box or sheet of plywood

A long table or smooth surface such as a garage floor.

Craft knife or a saw

What to do:

1. Before the party, you will need to cut the "cave" openings in the box or plywood. If using the plywood, cut as illustrated (fig. 15). Using a saw, cut the plywood in a half-oval shape with three openings at the bottom of various sizes. If necessary, make a support to hold the plywood up with the scrap wood, cut in triangles and nailed on. Now for the simple version: if using the box, remove any lids, so that when the box is turned upside down it is bottomless. Cut three openings at the front lower edge of the box.

2. During the party, prop or put the "cave" up on a table or set on a floor. Set it at one end of the table or floor with the openings facing the other end.

3. Give each child a turn to push the puck on the table or floor toward the openings on the board. Anyone getting the puck into the smallest opening gets a "special" prize. Anyone getting the puck into the larger openings gets a piece of candy. For very young children you might choose to let them keep on trying until they get it in.

Fig. 15. Board or box "cave" for Monkey Shuffle

Goin' on Safari

Now what would a Wild Jungle "Safari" Party be without an animal hunt?

You will need:

Small plastic animals
Paper bags

What to do:

1. Hide jungle-type plastic animals throughout your home or yard, especially in or under your plants. Don't hide them too deep in the "brush," — you don't want to be finding them a year from now when you trim your bushes. Put them where they can be seen.

2. After all of the animals have been hidden, hand the children a paper bag to hold their animals and tell the children that they are going on a wild animal safari. At the signal to go, send them out to search for their wild animals.

Watch That Snake!

You will need:

A jump-rope
A stopwatch or a watch with a second hand
A whistle

What to do:

1. Have two children sit down on the ground or floor. Give one end of the rope to one child, and the other end of the rope to the other child. They should be sitting far enough apart so that the jump-rope has just a little slack in it.

2. Choose a third child to stand next to the rope.

3. At the blow of the whistle the two seated children must begin wiggling the rope back and forth on the ground, like a snake. At the moment that they begin, the standing child must jump to miss the "snake." Any child to accidentally step on the snake before his 30 seconds are up is out. Winners may compete against one another until only one child is left. He is the winner.

Note: If the groups of children are of preschool age, make the time limit 15 seconds. If the children are older and more skilled at jumping rope, up the time limit according to their skill level.

Tarzan's Swinging Vine

You will need:

An old stuffed doll or a stuffed animal (e.g., a monkey)

2 long ropes

2 trees

A drawn target

Thumbtacks or tape

What to do:

1. Tie one of the ropes up high between two trees. Tie the other rope at the center of the one already up. The bottom of the hanging rope should be the average guest's chest height.

2. Pin or tape up the target on one of the trees.

3. Let the children take turns swinging the doll or stuffed animal. Anyone successful at hitting the target wins.

Hungry Monkey

You will need:

A large cardboard box

Acrylic paint

Craft knife

Plastic lids, such as margarine lids

What to do:

1. Before the party, cut an oval shaped hole on the box for the monkey's mouth. Paint a monkey face around it. Paint fruits (e.g., bananas, oranges, grapes, etc.) onto the lids.

2. During the party, line children up behind a marked line and give them three throws at the monkey's mouth. Whoever gets the most "food" into the monkey's mouth wins. An appropriate prize would be some fruit-type candy.

Lion Feed Toss

You will need:

A large piece of cardboard or a cardboard box

Scissors

Acrylic paint

A beanbag or a small ball

What to do:

1. Before the party, draw a lion onto the cardboard, making his mouth wide open, and cut out a mouth hole. Paint the lion. See illustration (fig. 16).

2. During the party, prop the piece of cardboard up against something like a picnic table, or anything that allows the ball or beanbag to go through. If using a box, just set it on the ground or on top of a table. Mark a throwing line about eight feet away from lion.

3. Have children stand in line and take turns throwing the small ball or beanbag into the mouth of the lion from a marked spot. Each child may have three turns. Whoever gets the most in wins. Allow preschoolers to keep throwing until they get one in.

Peanut Toss

You will need:

Three peanuts

A medium size bowl

A large piece of cardboard with an elephant painted on it, optional (see fig. 17)

A table or countertop

Fig. 16. Lion Feed Toss

What to do:

1. Place the bowl on a table or countertop. If using the picture of an elephant, place it in front of the table or countertop, and mark a throwing line from about eight feet away.

2. Line children up, and give each child three tosses of the peanuts. Write down each child's score after his turn. The one to get the most peanuts into the bowl wins a bag of peanuts.

Precaution: Do not use peanuts if children are under age three. They may choke on them.

Animal Charades

Divide the children into two equal teams. Have one child from each team go up in front of all the rest and pretend to be an animal. They may make sounds like the particular animal that you whisper in their ear or secretly

Fig. 17. Elephant

show them a picture of. Give the first team to guess the animal a point. Continue until all of the animals have been guessed. Use about 10 animals for a young group. Some animal examples are monkey, lion, bird, seal, snake, elephant, horse, rabbit, dog or cat.

Shaking the Banana Tree

See the Barnyard Party game "Shaking the Apple Tree." Replace the word "apple" with "banana."

Animal Mimic

Have a competition to see who can do the best animal imitation. An appropriate prize for this competition would be a birdcall instrument (found in sporting goods or nature stores).

☕ FAVOR AND ☕
PRIZE IDEAS

Zoo animal crackers, small plastic animals, gummy worms, spider rings, tangerines, items with jungle animals on them (e.g., pens, pencils, erasers, notebook pads, etc.), toy binoculars (or see Crafts, Safari Binoculars), Scary Tarantulas (see Craft), butterfly nets, animal books and coloring books, safari hats, Animal Masks (see Circus Party), drinking canteens and bananas.

Dinosaur Party

No bones about it, dinosaur parties never seem to go extinct. Children will always be fascinated with dinosaurs. One thing that I have noticed is that there always seem to be plenty of dinosaur themed party supplies. To me, that means that there is a demand. Maybe your child and his friends are fascinated with dinosaurs. At some point, I think every child is into them. Your party will be a roaring success if you choose to venture into the prehistoric unknown!

🎉 DINOSAUR 🎉 INVITATION

You shouldn't have much trouble finding a store-bought dinosaur invitation, but if you do, or if you just want to send one that is more creative than the typical store-bought invitation, make your own as illustrated on next page (fig. 18 a & b). You can even print a dinosaur invitation on your computer and just use the words shown.

🎉 DECORATIONS 🎉

- Decorate your mailbox with a dinosaur made out of construction paper. Hang green and yellow crepe paper and balloons from it and the front porch.

- Make dinosaur footprints out of construction paper. Place them along your sidewalk leading to your front door or backyard. Write a personalized "Hello" or "Welcome" to each guest. Stick the footprints to your sidewalk by putting a few loops of masking tape on the backside of each one. Face them so that guests can read them as they walk up your sidewalk.

- Hang long green crepe paper strips from the entrance to your porch. Guests must walk through the "jungle vines" to enter.

- Play a recording of jungle sounds on your front porch (check your local library, department store or music store). Play songs like "Crazy for

71

(a)

(b)

You're invited to a dino-mite Birthday Party for Daniel!

Don't be a bonehead, come on over. You're really going to dig this party.

Date: Saturday, May 10 A.D.
Time: 2pm – 4 pm
Place: 25 museum Ln
RSVP: 555–5555

Please wear your playclothes, because all little archeologists will be digging for dinosaur bones.

Fig. 18. Dinosaur Invitation

Dinosaurs" (Rosenshontz) or "If I Had a Dinosaur" (Raffi).

- Decorate the front door with a large dinosaur made out of construction paper.

- If you can get a large piece of cardboard, make a child size dinosaur and paint it. When guests arrive take their picture next to the dinosaur (maybe with their arm around it). The dinosaur could be holding a sign that reads something like, "Happy birthday Josh!"

- Bring any exotic plants that you may have from around the house into the party area.

- Decorate the party table with toy dinosaurs or stuffed dinosaurs. Add a few small potted plants for foliage.

- Drape lots of green crepe paper streamers across the ceiling of the party room to look like vines.

🎉 FOOD 🎉

- "Brontosaur-wiches"—peanut butter and jelly sandwiches cut with a dinosaur shaped cookie cutter.
- Dinosaur eggs—pitted olives. Show the children how to put them on their fingers—if they haven't already done so (they will, most likely, do this on their own).
- Prehistoric rock chips—your child's favorite potato chips.
- Raptor eggs—watermelon and cantaloupe balls or grapes.

Dinosaur Cake

You will need:

1 box of cake mix, plus ingredients as box directs

1 paper cupcake liner

2½ cups of green frosting

½ cup of blue frosting

Red gel frosting (found in tubes down the baking aisle of many grocery stores)

½ cup chocolate frosting
Toy dinosaurs and palm trees
Gummy fish, optional
Jellybeans for rocks or dinosaur eggs

What to do:

1. Mix batter as package directs. Pour a small amount of batter into the cupcake liner that has been set in a muffin pan. Pour the remaining batter into a greased and floured 9 × 13-inch pan.

2. Bake the cupcake about 20 minutes and bake the sheet-cake about 30 minutes.

3. Cool as directed. Cut the cup-cake to look like a volcano (cone shaped, with a flat top).

4. Place both the cake and the cupcake in the freezer uncov-ered for about an hour to make frosting easier.

5. Remove from freezer and frost the sheet cake green, leaving a spot for a "pond."

6. Frost the pond blue. If desired add gummy fish to the pond.

7. Place the cupcake on the cake with the large side down and frost it with the chocolate frost-ing for the volcano. For the lava on the volcano, frost red stripes down the side of the volcano with the red gel.

8. Place toy dinosaurs and palm trees on the cake.

9. Place jellybeans at the base of the palm trees for rocks or dinosaur eggs.

☆ CRAFTS ☆

Fossils

I made one of these crafts as a small child in kindergarten and my mother still keeps it with all of her memorable keepsakes. You just might like to do the same with your child's "fossil."

You will need:

Self-hardening clay (found at craft stores)
Waxed paper
A bowl approximately 6 inches in diameter
9 × 9-inch squares of cardboard, one square per child
A marker or pen
A rolling pin
A disposable cup filled with water
A few toothpicks
A straw
Ribbon or string

What to do:

1. Write each child's name on a square of cardboard, and place a sheet of waxed paper on top of the cardboard.

2. Place a large ball of clay on top of the waxed paper. Roll it out with the rolling pin to about a ½-inch in thickness.

3. Press the bowl, upside down, over the clay and cut as you would with a cookie cutter. Trim away the excess clay and reserve to use again.

4. Dip your fingers into the cup of water to wet them, and smooth the edges of the circle.

5. Lay the child's hand in the center of the clay, spreading out the fingers, and press down to create an imprint.

6. Poke a small hole at the top of the circle using the straw. This will create the hole for ribbon or string to be fed through when the clay is dry.

7. Carve the child's name and the date in the clay with the toothpick, and set it aside in a safe place until it is time for the guests to go home.

8. As the children leave to go home, hand them a ribbon for hanging the imprint. Explain to their parents that these must dry overnight and may be painted with acrylic paint when they are dry. They may be sprayed with clear acrylic gloss finish after the paint has dried. Tell them when the clear acrylic gloss dries to string the ribbon or string through the hole, and to tie a knot to secure it for hanging.

Note: You may have the children leave the "fossils" with you, so that you can paint them. Deliver the fossils with a thank you note.

Cave Drawings

You will need:

A library book that shows the children pictures of ancient pictographs, optional

A large blanket

A card table

Paper

Crayons or markers

Flashlights

Red and yellow tissue paper

What to do:

1. Before the party, decorate flashlights to look like caveman torches. Cut red and yellow tissue paper to look like flames and tape it to the flashlights.

2. Throw the blanket over the table with one end open to resemble the cave opening.

3. As guests arrive, have them draw a picture and have them hang their picture inside or outside of the cave.

4. Near the end of the party, or while guests are waiting for their food to be served, allow them to go cave exploring. If desired, place a piece of candy for each child in the cave.

🎉 GAMES AND 🎉 ACTIVITIES

Erupting Volcano

You can make a model volcano and use it as a centerpiece. When all of the guests sit down to eat, you can make it erupt.

You will need:

A large disposable aluminum baking pan

Small plastic bottle or flower vase with a small, narrow neck

½ cup vinegar

Red food coloring

Liquid dish detergent, optional

Baking soda, about ¼ cup or more

Sand and gravel

Funnel

What to do:

1. In a vinegar bottle mix vinegar, several drops of red food coloring, and dish detergent, if using.

2. Fill an empty soda bottle (cleaned and dry) or vase ½ full with baking soda, using the funnel for easier pouring. Place the bottle or vase in the center of the aluminum pan.

3. Pile gravel, then sand around the bottle to form the volcano. Be sure to leave the top of the bottle slightly exposed. Don't fill the sand too close to the edge of the pan. You will need a gap for the liquid to go into.

4. If desired, add some plastic dinosaur figures and palm trees to the sand around the volcano.

5. When all of the children are seated, tell them to watch the volcano erupt. Then pour the red vinegar mixture into the bottle or vase of baking soda and watch it erupt!

Note: If doing this activity indoors, cover the area with a plastic tablecloth to protect your table from any spills. Also, baking powder may be substituted for the baking soda, when necessary.

Take a Trip

If you have a dinosaur museum near your home, meet everyone there and tour the museum. Afterwards, bring everyone back to your home for a party.

Fossil Hunt

You will need:

Chicken, turkey, beef or other bones that would resemble dinosaur bones, or white cardboard

Scissors, if using cardboard

Small shovels

Old paintbrushes (the large kind used for painting walls)

Wire mesh sieve, optional (make a wood frame and hammer a screen onto it)

What to do:

1. Before the party, wash, scrub and boil the bones to sterilize them, or cut bone shapes from the cardboard. Hide the bones, leaving them partially exposed, in a sandbox, under leaves, dirt, pine straw or wood chips.

2. During the party, tell the children that they are paleontologists. Hand them small shovels and paintbrushes or the wire mesh sieve to help find the hidden bones. Let the children exchange their bones for prizes.

Dinosaur Egg Hunt

You will need:

Large fillable eggs, such as plastic Easter eggs that you may have stored away

Brown paint

Green paint

Egg fillers (e.g., dinosaur shaped fruit snacks, plastic toy dinosaurs or dinosaur stickers)

Bags for carrying eggs

Three cantaloupes, optional

Hay or straw, optional

What to do:

1. Before the party, paint the eggs brown, and let dry. Paint green dots or a camouflage look over the brown paint, and let dry. Fill the eggs with goodies, and hide the eggs in the yard or house, setting aside a couple of eggs for those who don't find any. If desired, lay the straw or hay somewhere on the ground outside, to look like a nest. If you have a wooded yard, somewhere underneath the trees would be great. Place the cantaloupes on top of the "nest."

2. During the party, pass out the bags and send the children to search for the hidden dinosaur eggs at the signal to go. Check to make sure that everyone has found some eggs. (You can oh-so-casually put the reserved eggs where you know those who haven't found any will find them.) All get to keep their plastic eggs that they find, but the cantaloupes are a reward to be shared by all and eaten.

Note: Reuse the straw or hay for planting grass seed in a needed spot of your yard, or use it to keep weeds down in the garden.

Dinosaur Guessing Contest

You will need:

Pictures of dinosaurs or toy dinosaurs

Pencils

Paper

What to do:

1. Set all of the pictures or toy dinosaurs on a table, and number them by putting a numbered slip of paper in front of each toy.

2. Pass out the pencils and paper, and tell everyone to number their paper. The children must write the name of the dinosaur that they think corresponds with the number. The one to guess the most correct wins. An appropriate prize would be a toy dinosaur.

Note: Most of the children who can write will get the spelling wrong. Do not count the spelling in this game. If it is close enough, count it as correct.

Flying Pterodactyls

See the Airplane Party game "Paper Airplane Landings."

Dinosaur Piñata

See the chapter on piñatas (end of book).

Dinosaur Egg Relay

If you will be using real eggs, this game will be messy and should be played outdoors and near the end of the party. If using real eggs, have a dozen on hand, just in case you should need them.

You will need:

Real uncooked eggs, hard-boiled eggs or plastic Easter eggs
Two spoons

What to do:

1. Divide the children into 2 equal teams and stand them behind a start line. Hand the first two children in line an egg and a spoon. Place a goal 20–30 feet away from the start line.

2. At the signal to go, the first child in line must place his egg on top of his spoon, run or walk as fast as he can to the goal, turn around and come back. If he drops the egg, he must pick it back up and replace it on the spoon before he may begin walking or running again. If you are using real eggs, and his egg cracks, he must get a new egg from an adult, who then passes it to him. The spoon must only be held by the handle.

3. Once he returns to his team, he passes the egg and spoon to the next child in line who must do the same as the first child. This continues until the first team to have all of its members finish wins.

♟ FAVOR AND ♟ PRIZE IDEAS

For a goody holder, decorate a paper bag with dinosaur stickers, stamps or stencils, or sponge-paint it with store-bought dinosaur shaped sponges.

Ideas for goodies: plastic dinosaur toys, dinosaur pencils, dinosaur shaped candy or fruit snacks, dinosaur stickers, dinosaur books, filled eggs (see Dinosaur Egg Hunt), plastic buckets with shovels, or straw hats like a paleontologist would wear.

Barnyard Party

Want to give a party that will give your guests something to crow about? You don't need to live on a farm to turn your home into a barnyard of bliss. Rent a movie such as *Charlotte's Web* to put you in the spirit, and watch it before the party. If you'd like to experience the real McCoy, you could even take your guests to a real farm to see actual farm animals or pick fruits and vegetables.

Whether you take your party on the road, or stay at home, this is a fun theme for any age group. This party will be a hit till the cows come home! No horsin' around!

OLD MACDONALD INVITATION

Ask guests to come dressed in their "farmer clothes." They could wear overalls, jeans, plaid shirts, jean shirts, straw hats, bandannas, etc. You can write your invitation as the one illustrated (fig. 19 a & b) or write one like the following example:

Front:
You're invited to a
   Barnyard
Birthday Party!

Back:
So come, let's flock
   together
Like birds of a feather!

DECORATIONS

- Decorate the mailbox, front porch, fence and party area with red and white balloons and crepe paper.

- Put a bale of hay in a red wagon and place near your front door. After guests have arrived, use the bale for the game "Needle in a Haystack." (Recycle the straw after the party by using it to hold down grass seed planted in bare spots of your lawn, or to keep weeds out of your garden.)

- For parties during the autumn season, you could put bundles of corn-

(a)

(b)

Old MacDonald had a farm, and on his farm he had lots of ......

FRIENDS!
You're invited to Valerie's Barnyard Birthday Party.
Date: Saturday, April 25th
Time: 11 a.m. - 1 p.m.
Place: Old Country Apple Orchard and petting Zoo 21 Orchard Lake Rd.
R.S.V.P. 555-5555

Lunch will be served. Please wear your farmer playclothes.

Fig. 19. Old MacDonald Invitation

stalks on each side of your front door. Place pumpkins, squash and gourds at the base of each stalk. This will look great for Halloween trick-or-treaters or Thanksgiving guests after the party, so these decorations can serve double duty!

- Make a scarecrow by stuffing an old shirt and pair of pants with straw or newspaper. Stuff a cloth or paper bag with newspaper for the head. Use a marker or paint to draw on a face. You can even attach buttons for the eyes and a nose. Place a straw hat on top. Place the scarecrow either at the front door or in the party area, by propping it upright against a wall or fence. You could even place it in your garden.

- Put a sign on your door or fence that reads, "Old MacDonald's Farm."

- Make pictures of farm animals or barns out of construction paper,

printed on a computer or from a coloring book, and hang around the party area.

- Decorate the party room with plastic or stuffed farm-type animals.

- Decorate the party table with a red and white checkered tablecloth, plates, cups and napkins. You might even choose to use blue tableware for more color.

- For a centerpiece, purchase plastic eggs that look like real chicken eggs (found in craft stores) and place them in a basket lined with a red and white checkered cloth napkin. Give each guest one to take home after the party is over. They make great pretend play toys.

- Some songs to play are "Old Mac-Donald," "Farmer in the Dell," "Grandpa's Farm" (Marcy Marxer), "Down on Grandpa's Farm" (Raffi), "Cluck, Cluck, Red Hen" (Raffi),

"Baa Baa Black Sheep" (Raffi), "Barnyard Dance" (John Mc-Cutcheon), "The Garden Song" (Maria Muldaur), "Six Little Ducks" (Joanie Bartels) and "Listen to the Land" (from the Official Album of Disneyland/Disney World).

Note: Most of these songs are for children about 6 and under.

🎉 FOOD 🎉

Pack a meal in a picnic basket and eat outside on a blanket or at a picnic table.

- Fried chicken, served warm or cold
- Cole slaw
- Potato salad or corn on the cob
- Hard boiled eggs or deviled eggs

Barnyard Cake

For a simple cake, decorate a sheet cake with green icing and make a pond with blue icing. Place plastic farm animal figures on the cake. If desired, put a Dutch windmill cookie on the green "grass."

Pig Cake

You will need:

1 box of cake mix, plus ingredients
   as box directs
10 paper cupcake liners
16 oz. can white frosting
Red food coloring
Assorted candies for decorating: red
   or black string licorice, M & M's,

chocolate chips, gumdrops and pink miniature marshmallows.
Vanilla wafers

What to do:

1. Grease and flour one 8- or 9-inch round cake pan. Prepare cake mix as directed on box. Pour 2½ cups batter into the round pan. Line muffin pan with liners and divide remaining batter equally into cups.

2. Bake cupcakes 20 minutes and bake round cake 30 minutes. Cool as directed. Freeze, if desired to make frosting spread easier.

3. To assemble, place round cake on a foil-covered board.

4. In a medium size bowl, stir 3 drops of red food coloring into frosting to make pink.

5. Spread frosting on top of one cupcake. Place it, frosting side down, on center of cake to form pig's nose.

6. Cut another cupcake in half vertically. Spread frosting on curved side of each half. For the ears, place the cupcake halves at the top edge of the cake, with the curved sides touching the cake as diagram shows (fig. 20).

7. Frost the rest of the cake pink, reserving some frosting for the remaining cupcakes and for the tongue.

8. Use vanilla wafers for the rounds of the eyes. Place a dab of frosting on the back of two M & M's of the same

Fig. 20. Pig Cake (with Cupcakes)

color, and stick on the center of each wafer for the eyes.

9. For the eyelashes, put 3 short pieces of licorice on top of each wafer.

10. For the nostrils on the snout, push two chocolate chips, point side down, into the top lower half of the nose.

11. Add a tiny drop of red food coloring to a small dab of frosting. Spread it on the round cake below the snout for a tongue.

12. Frost the remaining cupcakes with the reserved frosting. If desired, decorate them to look like little piglets.

🎉 CRAFTS 🎉

Animal Puppets

You will need:

Paper bags or old socks for hand puppets, or fingers cut from old gloves for finger puppets (if you don't have enough ask each guest to bring one)

Feathers

Pipe cleaners

Felt tip markers

Colored construction paper

Craft wiggle eyes

Glue

What to do:

1. Lay everything out on a table that is protected with a paper tablecloth or newspaper.

2. Let guests design their puppet any way they choose, using a paper bag, a finger from a glove or a sock as the animal body. Have one or two samples made for them to see.

Furry Little Sheep

You will need:

Pre-cut sheep body shapes (without legs) cut from white posterboard, 1 per child

Black felt tip markers

Precut black felt ears

White cotton balls

Glue

Clothespins, 2 per child

Craft wiggle eyes, 2 per child

Ribbon

Tiny metal bells (found at craft
stores)

What to do:

1. Lay out all of the items on a
   table that is covered with newspaper or a paper tablecloth.

2. Let the children assemble the
   sheep by gluing the cotton balls
   on the body (not the head) to
   resemble sheep's wool.

3. For the face, glue one eye and
   one ear onto each side of the
   head. Draw on a mouth.

4. Attach a bell around the neck
   with ribbon and tie it in place.

5. Clip the clothespins onto the
   lower half of the body for the
   legs.

Planting Seeds

You will need:

Foam cups, 1 per child

Masking tape

Pen or marker

Dirt, preferably bagged potting soil

A bucket, optional

A small shovel

A few large seeds such as bean seeds
or sunflower seeds

Sandwich bags, 1 per child

Rubber bands, 1 per child

What to do:

1. Before the party, label each
   child's cup with his name written on masking tape.

2. Pour the dirt into a bucket, if
   using, and stick a shovel in it.

3. Hand each child his cup and
   allow the children to take turns
   pouring scoops of dirt into
   their cups.

4. Hand them a few seeds to plant
   in the dirt. Afterwards, cover
   with a sandwich bag and secure
   with a rubber band.

5. Place cups near goody bags, so
   that you don't forget to send
   guests home with them. As
   guests leave to go home, remind them to remove the sandwich bags and water their seeds
   when they get home.

Animal Creations

Use the recipe below to make
modeling dough before the day of the
party. Store it in zippered plastic sandwich bags labeled with each child's
name. During the party, let the children shape it into their favorite farm
animal (e.g., cow, sheep, rooster, horse,
pig, etc.).

MODELING DOUGH RECIPE:

The following recipe makes one
medium size ball of dough, measuring
about 3½ inches in diameter. It may be
necessary to make a few batches, since
you cannot double this recipe.

You will need:

1 cup flour

½ cup salt

1 cup warm water

1 Tbsp. oil

1½ tsp. cream of tartar

Food coloring

What to do:

1. In a medium saucepan, add water, food coloring and oil. Stir and warm over medium-low heat.

2. As the mixture is warming (not boiling) mix flour, salt and cream of tartar.

3. Add flour mixture to water mixture and cook over medium heat , stirring constantly.

4. Cook 3–5 minutes or until mixture forms a ball in the center of the pan.

5. Remove from heat and cool in pan. Store in a sealed bag.

🎉 GAMES AND 🎉 ACTIVITIES

Take a Trip to a Farm

- If you know someone who owns a farm, ask them if they would mind your coming for a visit with the children. You may want to ask parents of younger children to stay and help you watch the children.

- Take a trip to a petting zoo. Many zoos have barnyards where they have demonstrations and hands-on experiences. I was surprised to learn that our local YMCA has a petting zoo. If you do not know of any, ask friends if they know of any. In some cities there are people who will bring farm animals to your home for a fee. If you live in a subdivision with a homeowners association, check to see if there are any prohibitions against this in the written bylaws.

- Check local newspaper ads or phone books to see if you have a farm nearby where you can take the children to pick their own fruits, such as apples, peaches, pumpkins, strawberries or blueberries. Many orchards have hayrides and demonstrations. If you have an orchard with a cider mill nearby, consider yourself very lucky. Take the children there, they'll love it.

- Some farms do birthday parties. My children once went to a great party at a farm. They played good old fashioned games, went on a hayride, petted the animals and roasted hot dogs over a campfire with sticks. It was a great time. My children still talk about it, and that was years ago.

- If food won't be available, check to see if any of these places have a picnic area that you can use. If not, bring a picnic blanket and eat on the ground or from a tailgate. You may even want to bring the party home afterwards, if you think that you or your guests will have any energy left.

Needle in a Haystack

You will need:

1 bale of hay or straw (check with a home improvement or hardware store)

Small inexpensive plastic toys (you can also use candy, but only very well wrapped candy)

1 large plastic needle (not a sharp needle)

What to do:

1. Loosely toss the hay or straw into a pile. Hide the toys or candy and plastic needle in the straw.

2. At the signal to go, let the children search through it for their toys or candy. The one who finds the needle is the winner.

Shaking the Apple Tree

1. All of the players stand in a circle. Choose one child to go in the center. The child in the center is the apple tree. Instruct him to cover his eyes.

2. Choose one of the children to gently shake the "apple tree" and return to his spot.

3. Once he returns to his spot all of the children chant, "Apple tree, apple tree, turn around. Apples, apples fall to the ground." This is the child in the center's cue to uncover his eyes, turn around and try to guess who shook him.

4. He gets three guesses. If he guesses wrong, the child who shook him gets a turn as the apple tree. If he guesses correctly he gets another turn as the apple tree. Play as long as you like, or until everyone has had a turn to be the apple tree.

Pass the Fruit

When I was a child we used to play a different version of this game at all of our family reunions. The way we used to play was to stick the orange under our chins to pass the orange. I saw this version at a birthday party, and decided that I like it better, although both ways are very fun.

You will need:

2 oranges

What to do:

1. Divide the children into two equal rows. Give the first child in each line an orange.

2. They are to place the orange between their elbows. At the signal, each must pass it to the child next to him, who must also take it between his elbows and pass it on down the line. If the fruit drops, the child must pick it up and continue passing it on down the line as before.

3. The first team to get their orange to the end of their line (between their elbows) wins.

Wishing Well

You will need:

A large wide-mouthed jar or a large coffee can filled with water

5 pennies per guest

What to do:

1. Place the jar on the ground, preferably just about 3 feet below a porch or deck with a secure railing. When the pennies drop in, they tend to splash a puddle around the jar or can, so this should be set up outdoors, if possible.

2. Allow the children to drop their pennies into the "Wishing Well." Anyone getting a penny in gets a wish for every penny. The one who gets the most into the jar wins a prize.

Doggie, Doggie, Where's Your Bone?

You will need:

Something to be the bone (e.g., dog bone snack, spoon, toy, chalkboard eraser, etc.)

What to do:

1. Choose one player to be the "doggie," and have him sit on a chair facing away from the other players. A "bone" is placed under his chair.

2. An adult quietly points to one of the other children, who are sitting in a semicircle on the floor or ground behind the "doggie." That player quietly sneaks up, takes the "bone," and returns to his spot on the floor.

3. Everyone then pretends to be holding the bone behind his own back, and they all chant, "Doggie, doggie, where's your bone? Someone's come and taken it home." The "doggie" then turns around and has to guess who took the bone. If you have a very young group, and a lot of children, give a few guesses. If he does not guess correctly, the other players identify the thief. Choose another child to be the "doggie,"

and the game continues. If time allows, play until each child has had a turn.

Kiss the Cow

You will need:

An empty soda bottle
A stuffed cow
A bowl
Chocolate kisses, 1 per child

What to do:

1. Seat all of the children in a circle and give each child a wrapped chocolate kiss.

2. Lay the bottle on its side in the center of the circle. Set the cow off to the side with the bowl next to it.

3. Going clockwise, each child takes a turn at spinning the bottle.

4. When the bottle stops spinning, the child who is sitting where the mouth of the bottle is pointing must give up a chocolate kiss to the stuffed cow by tossing it into the bowl. The game continues until only one child is left with a chocolate kiss. He is the winner and gets to keep all of the chocolate kisses.

Variation: Change this game to "Kiss the Pig" by using a stuffed pig.

Pin the Tail on the Donkey

This game can be purchased at many toy and party supply stores. You can even alter this game by pinning a tail on a cow, horse or pig.

Corn Relay

If you serve corn on the cob, the children can help prepare their meal by playing this game!

You will need:

1 unhusked ear of corn per guest

2 buckets

2 garbage cans

What to do:

1. Divide children into two equal teams and have them stand behind a marked line, single file.

2. About 20–30 feet from the marked line, put one ear of corn for each child into the bucket of his team. Count twice to be sure that you have one for each team member. Place a garbage can next to the bucket.

3. At the signal to go, the first child in each line must run to his team's bucket of corn, pick up an ear of corn, husk it completely, and run back. He touches off the next teammate in line who runs and does the same. The first team to finish husking all of their corn and return back wins.

Corn Toss

You will need:

A bucket

10 unpopped popcorn kernels

Pencil and paper

What to do:

Line the children up behind a marked line and have them take turns tossing 10 grains of corn into the bucket. Write down how many each child gets into the bucket. The child to get the most in wins a prize. An appropriate prize would be a box of caramel popcorn.

Know Your Seeds

See the Jack in the Beanstalk Party game "Know Your Beans." Use ordinary, easily recognized seeds such as watermelon, cucumber, apple, and orange seeds.

Animal Charades

See Wild Jungle Safari Party (use farm animal sounds).

Round-Up

See Wild West Party.

Pig Piñata

See chapter on piñatas (end of book).

🎉 FAVOR AND 🎉 PRIZE IDEAS

Seed packets, small rakes, small shovels, baskets of fruit, Cowtails candy sticks, bandannas, straw hats, plastic farm animal figures, coloring books of farm animals, animal shaped cookies, Jolly Rancher candy, Furry Little Sheep (see Crafts), Animal Puppets (see Crafts), pots with planted seeds (see Crafts) or Animal Creations (see Crafts).

Wild West Party

Bring the spirit of the old west alive with this party. If your little cowpoke loves western movies, western music, panning for gems, cowboy clothing or horses, he's going to have a great time. Choose this party, pardner, and you'll transport your child and his friends back in time to the good old days of the "Wild West." Lasso up some friends and get ready for some foot stompin' fun! Yee haw!

⛏ WESTERN ⛏ INVITATION

Mail an invitation like the one shown in the illustration (fig 21 a & b), or make wanted posters on parchment paper and have your child hand deliver them to friends all decked out in his sheriff costume. For the wanted posters you could photocopy each guest's picture from a school yearbook, cut it out and glue it onto the invitation. At the top of the invitation write,

"WANTED!" Underneath the photocopied picture write the child's name and something like, "And all of Tony's friends for his Wild West birthday party!" Add the date, time, place, and your phone number, and finish with, "Please join us for some wild western rodeo games and some chuck wagon grub. Please wear your western duds!"

⛏ DECORATIONS ⛏

Most party supply stores sell decorations with a western theme. If you are unable to find any, use some of the following suggestions:

- Decorate the mailbox, front porch and party area with brown, black and red balloons and crepe paper.

- Draw a picture of a cowboy on a large piece of cardboard and paint or color it. Put it on the front door or gate. Make pictures of green cactus, black horseshoes, yellow cowboy hats, yellow stars and brown horses.

(a)

Howdy Pardner

It's Roundup Time !

(b)

We're celebratin' 'cause Nicole is
turnin' 9. So saddle up your horse
and come on over, we're havin' a
Wild Western Birthday Bash!
This here's the date: Sun., march 15
A raindate has been set for mar.22
See ya'll about: 3:30pm - 6:00 pm
Over yonder at: 21 wagontrain Rd.
Kindly RSVP: 555-5555
Please wear your western duds
(cowboy hats will be provided).
Thank you kindly ya'll!
Supper will be provided by the
trail boss and the cook (mom & Dad)
along with fun and games.

Fig. 21. Western Invitation

Make the pictures out of construction paper or make them on a computer and hang them in the party area.

- Make a banner that reads, "WESTERN ROUND-UP" and hang it on a fence or in the party room.

- Make wanted signs with each child's photocopied yearbook picture on them. Hang on the walls in the party room or on a fence. Let the children take them home as party favors.

- Make signs that look like wood using cardboard and black paint. Write location names like "Boot Hill," "O.K. Corral," "Saloon," "Western Trail," "Gold Mine" or "Watering Hole." Hammer the signs to wooden stakes and pound the stakes into the ground, being careful not to hit any power lines.

- Use a red and white checkered tablecloth. Use blue plates, cups and napkins. You could even use tableware with a western theme.

- For a centerpiece, stick a cowboy hat in the center of the table. Hide candy under it. Give a piece to each child as they arrive. During the party, use the hat to hold prizes to be passed out. You could also use a toy train or a battery powered camping lantern for a centerpiece.

- If you have a playhouse in your yard, put a sign on it that reads, "Town Jail" or "Saloon." For the jail, put cardboard strips on the windows to resemble jail bars. Take a picture of each child in the "jail."

- Decorate the party area with toy wagons filled with straw or hay (which could be used for the Needle in a Haystack game), a rocking horse (which could be used for the Cattle Ropin' game), or even a spring-type hobby horse.

- Fill a tub with ice and put cans or bottles of root beer in it. Stake the "Watering Hole" sign behind it.

- Some of the following songs can be found at your local library or music store. See if a friend or relative has some of the oldies, but goodies. Some songs to play are "Old Dan Tucker" (Dan Dalton), "Cindy" (Dan Dalton), "Skip to My Lou"

(Dan Dalton), "She'll Be Coming 'Round the Mountain" (Dan Dalton), "Yellow Rose of Texas" (Dan Dalton), "Put Your Little Foot" (Tex-I-An Boys), "Cattle Call" (LeAnn Rimes and Eddy Arnold), "The Greatest Hits Collection CD" (Brooks and Dunn), "Big Iron" (Marty Robbins), "Leavin' Cheyenne" (Ian Tyson), "Mule Train" (Frankie Lane and the Muleskinners — this one is great for the game Horse Relay!), "Jingle Jangle Jingle" (Tex Ritter and His Texans), "Lovenworth" (Roy Rogers), or "Maple Leaf Rag" (this is a wonderful saloon-type piece found on the Official Album of Disneyland/Disney World). All are great songs!

🎉 FOOD 🎉

Cowboys cooked their food in iron pots over open campfires, and they ate their food out of tin plates. While on the trail, they lived mainly off of beans, rice, potatoes, biscuits and coffee. If they were lucky and they had a good cook, they were served pudding and an occasional pie — the last piece usually being fought over. After living off such a menu, I would imagine a trip to town was quite exciting! We'll try to jazz the menu up just a little, but if you stick with the Open Pit Grub menu it will be more authentic.

Chuck Wagon Grub

This here's some fixin's that will tame the wildest little cowpoke after a hard day on the trail ... until they fight over the last piece of meat!

- Barbecued chicken or ribs, or gold nuggets (chicken nuggets)
- Iron skillet potatoes
- Wagon wheel pasta salad
- Tumbleweed salad (greens)
- Biscuits
- Long necked bottles or cans of root beer, or mouth puckerin' lemonade

Open Pit Grub

For y'all adventurous trail bosses, make a campfire (check local fire ordinance laws). Coleman makes a great portable outdoor firepit for those who don't have a firepit. Make roasting sticks (one for each person) out of long tree sticks. With a sharp scout knife or a pocketknife, cut a pointed tip on one end of each (an adult must do this). Clean the pointed stick end with a damp paper towel. One great way to make a firepit is to use curved landscape retaining wall bricks. Mine are stacked 3 high into a circle. Around my pit I have 12 (the perfect number of guests for a party) wooden tree stumps from a tree that died on my property. I've preserved them with marine varnish. Before the party, I send my children around the yard to pick up kindling (fallen pinecones, small sticks and bark) and we toss it into the pit until needed, along with a couple of logs. We always make sure that we have plenty of adult supervision around the fire. We keep a bucket of water and a hose ready to douse any flames. The food on an open pit is some mighty fine eatin'! You can eat on aluminum pie plates if you like. Go ahead, be adventurous, it's fun!

- Hot dog, two per guest
- Hot dog buns, two per guest
- Condiments: mustard, ketchup, etc.
- Pork and beans (heat this in the house and serve in small disposable bowls)
- Potato chips
- Marshmallows for roasting (careful, they catch on fire easily), optional
- Cans of root beer or mouth puckerin' lemonade

S'mores

You will need:

Marshmallows
Graham crackers
Chocolate candy bars

What to do:

1. To make the S'mores, let the children roast their marshmallow to a light brown color, turning it so that it does not burn. Don't let the marshmallow touch the flames — it will catch on fire and need to be doused in the bucket of water, ruining it. An adult will need to help the children make these.

2. Pull the marshmallow off the stick by squeezing it between 2 graham cracker squares. This will keep your hands clean.

3. Sandwich a square of chocolate in between the 2 graham crackers. Delicious!

Horse Cake

You will need:

1 box of cake mix, plus ingredients as box directs
3 cups chocolate frosting
1 cup white frosting
Assorted candies: red or black shoestring licorice, a black jellybean, LifeSavers candies and one small round M & M candy (green or brown)

What to do:

1. Using a 9 × 13-inch pan, bake and cool the cake as directed. Cut as shown in diagram (fig. 22a). If desired, freeze uncovered for about an hour to make the frosting spread more easily.

2. Remove from freezer and set on a foil-covered board. Place the ear on top of the head.

3. Frost the entire cake with chocolate frosting.

4. Use the white frosting and a round decorating tip for the mane. Pull the tip at the end of each hair strand (without squeezing the frosting bag) to give it a pointed look.

5. Frost on a white eye, by swirling the frosting in an oval shape. Top with an M & M candy.

6. Braid the licorice to create the bridle and reins. Connect them with 2 LifeSavers candies and 2 single strands of licorice as shown in diagram (fig. 22b).

7. Use a jellybean for the nostril and a single strand of licorice for the mouth.

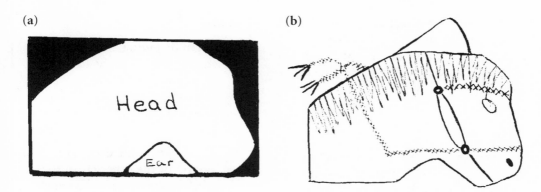

(a)   (b)

Fig. 22. Horse Cake

Corral Cake

You will need:

1 box of cake mix, plus ingredients as box directs

1 16-oz. can butterscotch frosting or 2 cups light brown frosting

1 16-oz. can blue frosting (or one can white tinted blue)

Thin pretzel sticks, optional

Plastic cowboy and Indian figures

What to do:

1. Using a 9 × 13-inch pan, bake and cool cake as directed. If desired, freeze for about one hour or more to make frosting easier.

2. Frost with butterscotch or light brown frosting, leaving a space unfrosted for a stream or watering hole.

3. Use the blue frosting to make the stream or watering hole.

4. Make a corral fence by standing thin pretzel sticks in the cake edge in a criss-cross fashion.

5. Decorate the inside of the cake with plastic cowboy and Indian figures.

6. Stack a few more pretzel sticks on the cake to look like a campfire. If desired, stick a lit candle in the center of the pretzels. Just don't let the flames get too close to the pretzels — they could burn!

Pretend Campfire

Want a campfire but can't have one? (Maybe there's a ban on burning, or it's raining outside, or you live in an apartment.) Don't be discouraged; just build a pretend campfire, indoors or outdoors.

For an indoor campfire make "logs" by covering cardboard oatmeal containers or cans with brown paper (brown paper bags or brown construction paper will work). Glue the paper on. Set a few of these "logs" on the floor in a pile. Use covered paper towel tubes for pretend kindling. Crumple some yellow, orange and red tissue paper for flames and set them on top. You can also use construction paper and cut it into flame shapes. Glue it onto the pretend logs. Turn out the lights and prop flashlights around the "fire," being careful not to let the flashlights get too close to the paper.

To make an outdoor pretend fire, make a circle with medium sized rocks and put sticks and wood in the center of the circle. Make pretend flames as with the indoor campfire.

Pitch a Tent

Whether you have a sleepover or not, you can set up a tent. If you don't have a tent, use a drop cloth or an old sheet. Stretch a rope or clothesline between two trees or poles and tie it tightly. Drape the drop cloth or sheet over the rope or clothesline. Anchor the sides with rocks or logs.

Arrival of Guests

As guests arrive, put a cowboy hat, bandanna and sheriff's badge on everyone. Make paper star sheriff's badges out of yellow paper. Write names on them and use them as nametags. Write "sheriff" on the birthday child's badge, and write "deputy" on everyone else's. Attach with a safety pin or tape.

CRAFTS

Log Cabins

You will need:

Popsicle sticks (large boxes of them can be purchased at craft stores. Buy plenty; return what isn't used.)

Glue

Hot glue (only an adult may use this)

What to do:

1. Begin by gluing 4 sticks into a square. The 2 on the left and right go on the bottom. Place 2 more sticks on the top, creating a square, and glue the ends together.

2. Continue gluing each layer, one on top of the other, as in step 1. The children may go as much as 3 inches high.

3. Make a roof by laying some sticks out, side by side. Hold them together by gluing two sticks crossways on top of the row of sticks. Place one on each end. This step works best if it is hot-glued by an adult. A pointed roof can be made with two of these pieces, but for a party keep it simple and make a flat roof.

GAMES AND ACTIVITIES

Go Horseback Riding

If the children are old enough, consider taking them horseback riding. Use a reputable riding stable. (I like to use the YMCA.) At our local stable the horses are fairly calm and gentle. At most YMCAs they also have picnic areas that you can reserve for an outdoor party. You will need to go to the stables to pick up permission slips for the parents to sign. We send ours out with the invitations and ask parents to bring them the day of the party. Have extra permission slips on hand for those who forget to bring theirs. The children will be required to wear a riding helmet at most stables. If the children have a horseback riding helmet of their own, they should be able to use it. Always make any reservations well in advance and call to confirm them.

Tall Tales

Cowboys are great storytellers. Whenever cowhands get together, they are likely to tell tall tales, usually around the nightly campfire. Many of these stories have become part of our American folklore. Find some good American Western folklore books and read them to the children around the campfire (real or pretend).

You could also seat all of the children in a circle around the campfire and let them make up scary ghost stories to tell. You'll hear some good ones, I'm sure. If it is dark enough outside, allow each child to put a flashlight up to his face for a spooky effect. If it is too dark outside to videotape the story telling, use a tape recorder, so that you may listen to it years from now.

Calming the Herd

Music was usually played on a harmonica, banjo or fiddle before bedtime. Traditional cowboy songs were sung by the night watchman during roundup time. They sang to calm the herd of sleeping cattle as they slowly rode around the herd. Maybe a song or two will calm your restless herd. If you (or a relative or friend) are musically talented, you could play some cowboy songs around the campfire on a guitar, banjo, harmonica or fiddle. Teach the children some western songs. Copy sheet music for children who are old enough to read, and encourage them to sing by showing them how. You may even want to have a square dance or country line dance. Get a book or video from the library on the subject to learn some steps to teach the children, or take them to a country western dance club on family night.

Giddy Up!

Let preschool aged children ride a hobbyhorse for one minute each.

Horse Relay

You will need:

2 stick-type wooden horses or 2 brooms

A whistle, or western music with songs such as "Mule Train" or "She'll Be Comin' 'Round the Mountain"

What to do:

1. Line the children up in 2 lines. Tell the first child in each line to put the horse or broom between his legs as if riding it.

2. At the blow of the whistle or the start of the music, they must hop or run to a marker, about 20–30 feet away, then come back.

3. The first 2 children then pass the "horse" to the next teammate in line. The second child in each line does the same as the first child. Keep the music playing all the while, if used. This continues until all of one

team's players finish. They are declared the winning team.

Round-up

A familiar trademark of the cowboy was a brightly colored bandanna, folded and tied around his neck. The bandanna could be used to protect his neck from sunburn. During round-ups and trail drives, it could be pulled over his face as a dust mask. It had many other uses too, but I wonder if they ever used it to play this old game.

You will need:

1 bandanna

What to do:

1. Have all of the children but one form a circle.
2. Hand the bandanna to the child outside the circle and have him walk around the circle. He must drop the bandanna behind one of the children.
3. The one who the bandanna is dropped behind must pick up the bandanna and start chasing the bandanna-dropper around the circle, trying to tag him before the dropper goes all the way around the circle and enters the vacant spot. If the chaser catches the dropper, then the dropper must go in the corral — that is, the center of the circle — and the chaser becomes the next bandanna-dropper. If the chaser cannot catch the dropper, then the chaser must go into the corral, and the original dropper gets to "drop" again.

4. The only way to get out of the corral is to grab the bandanna from behind someone where it has been dropped before that person gets it. End this game whenever you wish, or when there are so many children in the corral that the game cannot continue.

Fast Draw

You will need:

A toy gun or water gun

A holster

A handkerchief

What to do:

If the children have their own toy guns and holsters, they can use these. If not, let them take turns using one (with their parents' permission). Have them take turns dropping a handkerchief with their left hand in front of their face. See if they can catch it with their gun in their right hand at waist high. After a few tries all will be pros. If you want to make this a contest, do this "before" they have all been practicing.

Variation: The children may use a pointed finger instead of a toy gun.

Panning for Gold

You will need:

Cleaned small rocks

Gold spray paint

Newspaper

Beach sifter or an old kitchen strainer that you no longer need

Shovels

A sandbox or pile of "fine" sand

Plastic zippered bags, one per child,
labeled with names

Bucket of water, optional

What to do:

1. Before the party, lay out the
   newspaper (outdoors), place the
   rocks on top of it and spray
   paint them. Dry the rocks. Flip
   them over and paint the other
   side.

2. Hide this "gold" in the sandbox
   or pile of sand, but not too
   deep, or it will be too hard to
   find.

3. During the party, have the children take turns scooping up
   some sand with the shovel and
   pouring it into the sifter. Let
   them sift the sand through the
   sifter to find some gold. Let
   them have more scoops if they
   can't find any gold, but makes
   sure that no one takes too
   much. Save some for others.

4. Have them rinse their gold in
   the bucket of water, put it into
   their bags, and seal it shut.

Variation: You can make a sifter
by constructing a square wooden frame
(or using an old picture frame) and
nailing a screen to it.

Note: This activity is messy. If you
choose to do it, warn the parents on
the invitation to send the children in
play clothes. For parties with very
young children, keep some clean rocks
hidden in your pocket. Sneak some
rocks into their scoop without them
seeing you do it, if they are having
difficulty finding any.

Shoot Out at the O.K. Corral

Better be ready to defend your ter-
ritory, pardner, 'cause you're about to
take some hits!

You will need:

Two long ropes or pieces of string of
equal length

"Ammunition" (crumpled paper
balls or foam balls)

A stop watch or kitchen timer

What to do:

1. Place the ropes on the ground
   or floor, parallel to one another.
   They should be 8 to 10 feet
   apart. If you will be playing
   outdoors and it is windy make
   them closer.

2. Divide the children into two
   equal teams, one being the
   "law" and the other being the
   "outlaws." Have each team
   stand behind their string.

3. Give each child a crumpled ball
   of paper. At the signal to go,
   start the timer for 1 minute.
   They must all try to throw their
   "ammunition" across the other
   team's rope. They all continue
   throwing the balls again and
   again until 1 minute is up.

4. Tell them to stop and count the
   ammunition on their side of
   the rope. The team with the
   least ammunition wins.

Gold Rush Hunt

There's gold in them there hills!

You will need:

"Gold" (gold foil-covered chocolate [kisses or coins], gold plastic coins or yellow bubble gum)

Plastic sandwich bags or cellophane

Yellow wrapping paper ribbon

Paper bags, one per guest, labeled with children's names

What to do:

1. Before the party, wrap the "gold" in squares of cellophane or place in bags. Put a few pieces in each and tie closed with ribbon.

2. The day of the party, hide the candy in the yard or house.

3. Give each child a paper bag to hold their "gold." At the signal to go, send them out prospecting!

Stampede

Have a race with all of the children at one time. Line them up behind a starting line. At the signal to go, all race to a finish line. The first one to get to the finish line wins.

Cattle Ropin'

There are many ways that you can make or play this game. Use a hobbyhorse, rocking horse or a large stuffed animal if you have one. Just use your own imagination. If something that you have around the house is more convenient, use it. Below are some ideas that some cowboys and younguns actually use.

You will need:

- A cow body: a cardboard box, a bale of straw, a wooden sawhorse, or a log with 4 boards nailed on for legs.

- A head: a cardboard or wooden steer-shaped head, or a tin coffee can with two holes in it and a pipe or stick stuck through the holes for horns (hammer down any sharp edges).

- A lariat: A long rope with a slip knot (a sliding noose) at one end with the rope slipped through the loop, or a hula-hoop with a rope tied to it.

- Something to secure the head to the body: rope, nails or screws.

What to do:

1. Before the party, attach the head to the body that best suits the body that you have chosen.

2. During the party, stand the children behind a marked spot about 10–15 feet back from the steer.

3. Let them take turns throwing the rope and trying to lasso the steer head. Each child may have three turns to throw the rope.

Cow Hunt

You will need:

Longhorn shapes made from brown paper or printed on a computer

Pen

What to do:

1. Before the party, write a point amount on the back of each longhorn (e.g., 5, 10 or 15).

2. Hide the shapes indoors or outdoors.

3. Divide the children into two teams and send the cowpokes out to find some cattle!

4. When they have found all of the cattle, total each team's score. The team with the highest score wins.

Cow Branding

Ranchers organized cow hunts in which cow-hunters or cowhands would capture wild longhorns and brand them for the ranch owners. This is how ranchers first built up their herds. Play this game as you would regular tag. Any child to be tagged by "it" or the "cowboy" must go to the corral. A garage works well as the corral.

Blind Man's Bluff

This is a very old game that dates back to the 14th century, and was also played by the pioneer children. In Austria the game is called Blind Cow.

You will need:

A bandanna or a blindfold

What to do:

1. Blindfold one child and put him into the center of a circle of children.

2. Spin him around a few times.

3. The player then must catch someone and figure out who it is. The other players may dis-

guise their voices and pretend to be someone else.

4. The child to be recognized then becomes the next "blind man."

Dice

If you have a child's pool table, let the children take turns rolling a set of dice onto the table. The highest score wins.

Horseshoes

A game of horseshoes can be purchased at many toy stores and department stores.

Pin the Tail on the Donkey

This game can be purchased at many toy and party supply stores, or you can make your own game out of cardboard or construction paper. You can even alter this game by pinning a tail on a steer or a horse.

Needle in the Haystack

See Barnyard Party.

🎉 FAVOR AND 🎉 PRIZE IDEAS

Red bandannas, sheriff badges, inexpensive straw cowboy hats, plastic cowboy and Indian figures, gold foil-covered chocolate coins, gold nuggets (gold painted rocks), Hershey's Nugget candy bars and gold foil-covered chocolate kisses, Big League Chew bubble gum, bags of yellow nugget gum, Jolly Rancher candy, Cowtails candy sticks, beef jerky, horse-shaped cookies, harmonicas, train whistles, handcuffs, horseshoes, rubber toy snakes, canteens, water guns or Log Cabins (see Crafts).

Fishing Party

Are you fishin' for a unique party? Consider taking your child and his friends on a fishing trip. Of course living near a lake, pond, river or ocean really isn't essential to having a fishing party. With the ideas listed here in this chapter, your child and his friends will feel like they have spent the day fishing whether you take them on a real or pretend fishing trip. If your child loves to go fishing, or recently caught his first fish, you may have hooked the right party with this chapter!

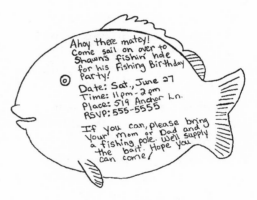

Fig. 23. Fish Invitation

🎉 FISH 🎉 INVITATION

Make a fish invitation like the one shown in the illustration (fig. 23). Use bright yellow or red paper as an attractive bait, and reel your guests on in!

🎉 DECORATIONS 🎉

- Put green and blue balloons and crepe paper on the mailbox, front porch and in the party area.

- Decorate your front door with a fish made of construction paper, or make a sign that reads, "Welcome aboard, mates!"

- Twist green crepe paper to look like seaweed and hang from blue streamers.

- Hang fishing bobbers from the ceiling with fishing line.

- Put fish shapes on the walls and doors. Hang some from the ceiling with fishing line.

- If you already own fishing gear, decorate your home with it.

- If you own a rowboat, place it in the yard. Let the children get in it and pretend that they're fishing or rowing the boat.

- Try to find a paper tablecloth and tableware with fish on it. You could also use a blue tablecloth (as water). Cut fish shapes from colorful paper and tape them to the tablecloth. Use blue and green tableware.

- Put plastic fish, toy boats, real seashells or even a fishbowl with real fish in it on the table.

- Play songs like "Row, Row, Row" (Raffi), "Octopus's Garden" (Raffi or the Beatles), "Fishin' Blue" (Shake Sugaree), "Goin' Fishin'" (Rosenshontz), "Wynken, Blynken and Nod" (Joanie Bartels), "Closer to Home (I'm Your Captain)" (Grand Funk Railroad), "Rock the Boat" (W. Holmes), "Shiver Me Timbers" (Bette Midler) or "Rock Lobster" (B52's). The first five songs listed are primarily for younger children.

⛺ FOOD ⛺

If taking your party on the road, bring plenty of wet wipes for everyone to wash their hands with. Bring a garbage bag to throw your trash in. Bring along a cooler with some ice to keep everything cold.

- I Could Eat a Whale Sandwich: cut bread with a fish shaped cookie cutter and fill with tuna fish salad.

- Fish shaped crackers.

- Celery Boats: fill celery stalks with peanut butter and stick a corn tortilla into the peanut butter as a sail

- Canned drinks (if going fishing) or Blue Lagoon Drinks (at home): Blue colored drinks with gummy fish ice cubes floating in them (fill ice cube trays with gummy fish, pour blue drink over them and freeze). Tell the children to be careful not to swallow the gummy fish, if they fall out of the ice cubes.

Fish Cake

You will need:

1 box of cake mix, plus ingredients as box directs

Blue cellophane, optional

4 cups of frosting (any color)

½ cup of frosting in a different color, optional

Shoestring licorice, optional

Small round candy or chocolate chip for the eye

Gummy fish, optional

What to do:

1. Using a 9 × 13-inch pan, bake and cool the cake as directed. Cut the cake as diagram shows (fig. 24a) and freeze uncovered for about an hour to make the frosting spread more easily.

2. Remove the cake from the freezer and assemble on a foil-covered board that also has been covered with blue cellophane. Assemble as diagram shows (fig. 24b). Move the triangle piece to the opposite end to make the head. Turn the two side pieces around to make the fins.

3. Frost with any color icing you choose, maybe your child's favorite color. If you like, frost the body and fins one color and frost the face another color. Use the color that was used on the face to pipe on the details such as scales, fins and mouth, or use shoestring licorice to make the details.

4. Put a piece of candy or chocolate chip on for an eye.

5. Put a few gummy fish on the "water" (the blue cellophane).

🎉 CRAFTS 🎉

Fishing Hats

Supply everyone with a fishing hat. Put some fabric paint, lures without hooks and safety pins on a table, and let the children decorate a fancy fishing hat. Hook the lures onto the hat with safety pins.

Fishing Poles

The children will use these for the game Hook the Fish, if you plan on playing it. If you don't want to have the children each make one of these, you will need to make one for the game.

You will need:

3-foot sticks or wooden dowels (about ½-inch in diameter), 1 per guest
String
Small brass rings, 1 per guest
A drill
Felt tip markers, optional

(a)

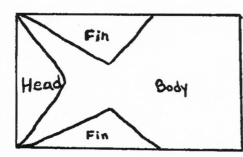

(b)

Fig. 24. Fish Cake

What to do:

1. Before the party, drill a hole at the tip of each dowel or stick, just big enough for the string to fit through. Write the children's names on the poles.

2. During the party, have the children decorate their poles with felt tip markers. Let each child thread about a 2½–3 foot piece of string through the stick hole and knot it. Have them tie a brass ring to other end of the string and you have a fishing pole ready to hook a prize fish!

Japanese Fish Kites

Kite flying is very popular all over Asia and is linked to many ancient traditions. On Children's Day in Japan (May 5th) Japanese children hang kites in the shape of carp outside their homes. When the wind blows, the fish shaped kites fill with air and look as if they are swimming. The carp stands for energy, strength, and a long life.

You will need:

Paper or fabric

Scissors

A hole puncher

Strips of cardboard and a cardboard fish shaped template

Glue

String

Wooden dowels, bamboo sticks or even straight sticks from your yard

Felt tip markers or paint

What to do:

1. Fold a piece of paper or fabric over to form a rectangle. Draw the outline of a fish with a wide mouth as shown in illustration (fig. 25). Have a template made of cardboard for the children to trace a fish shape from. Let them cut out the fish shape.

2. Glue the sides of the fish together, leaving the mouth and tail ends open for the wind to blow through.

3. Cut a thin strip of cardboard to fit around the inside of the mouth. The cardboard should be in a ring shape. Make two holes with the hole puncher, one on each side of the mouth. Glue and let dry.

4. Draw or paint scales and fins on the fish.

5. Thread string through the holes in the mouth. Attach the other end of the string to a stick or dowel. Now your kites are ready to swim in the breeze!

Caution: Keep away from power lines.

Fig. 25. Japanese Fish Kite

☙ GAMES AND ☙ ACTIVITIES

Boat Rides

If you live on or near a lake or pond, take the children out on a boat. If the boat is a rowboat, give each child a chance to row the boat. Only take two children out at a time. If the boat is large, have their parents come out on the boat and take more children. Of course, follow the guidelines for the number of people allowed on the boat and make sure that everyone is wearing a life jacket. Try and take everyone out for the same amount of time, to avoid any hurt feelings or to avoid keeping anyone waiting too long.

Fishing

If you live on or near a lake or pond, ask guests to bring a fishing pole or allow them to use one of yours. Let them actually fish. Supply the bait for your guests and hook it for them. It would be a good idea for their parents to stay and help if you will be doing this activity. You will need plenty of extra help not only watching the children, but helping them hook the bait and casting the lines. Remind the children that a fishing hook is very sharp and could hurt someone. Only allow an adult to cast the lines. Never leave guests unattended, not even for a minute. Bring along a first aid kit, just in case. Bring plenty of wet wipes to wash hands and a garbage bag to dispose of trash in.

Skipping Stone Contest

If your party will be held near a lake, pond or stream, have a skipping stone contest. See who can get the most skips from a stone by throwing it into the water. The stones should be thrown sideways or sidearm (not over or underhand). Have an adult show the children how to make the stones skip. Make sure that they don't throw them at one another, just at the water. Write down how many skips each child gets. The child to get the most skips from his stone is the winner.

Caution: Keep a close eye on the children, so that no one falls into the water. If necessary, have extra help.

Feed the Fish

You will need:

A piece of wood or cardboard
Paint
A drill, jigsaw or craft knife
3 beanbags (preferably with fish painted on them)

What to do:

1. Cut holes approximately 5 inches in diameter into your board, using the drill and jigsaw for a wood board, and the craft knife if using the cardboard. Make anywhere from 3 to 5 holes.

2. Paint fish around the holes, making the holes look like the mouths of the fish. Paint green seaweed, blue water and white bubbles coming from the mouths of the fish. Paint score numbers onto each fish giving some 5 points and some 10

points. If you like, make one 20 points.

3. Line the children up behind a marked line about 6 feet away and have them take turns tossing the beanbags into the fish mouths. As each child gets one into the hole, write down his score. Tally up each child's score and declare the one with the highest score the winner.

Man Overboard

You will need:

One hula-hoop

A long rope

A cardboard box, doll or stuffed animal (smaller than the circumference of the hula hoop)

What to do:

1. Attach the rope to the hula-hoop.

2. Place the cardboard box, doll or stuffed animal approximately 7–8 feet from a marked tossing point.

3. Allow children to toss the hoop and try to ring the box, doll or stuffed animal. They get three throws. If they hoop it, they win a prize. A roll of LifeSavers candy would be a very appropriate prize.

Fish Guess

You will need:

Easily recognized pictures of different fish, such as animal cards or pictures printed from a computer

(e.g., catfish, shark, swordfish, goldfish, starfish, etc.)

Paper, 1 sheet per guest

Pencils, 1 per guest

What to do:

1. Before the party, cover any names of the fish that might show and number each picture.

2. During the party, hand each guest a pencil and paper. Let them guess what each fish is, and then write it down on their piece of paper in the correct numerical order. An adult can write the guesses for children too young to write. The one who correctly guesses the most wins a prize.

Hook the Fish

This is a game played at fairs in England during the summer. It is much like the Magnetic Fish Pond Game played at many fairs and carnivals. Instead of having a magnet attached to the end of the string it has a ring, and instead of a paperclip being attached to a paper fish it has a hook attached to a wooden fish. If cutting the wood is too much trouble, play the traditional way, but the hook is much more fun and can be played many more times after the party is over.

You will need:

1 fishing pole from the craft Fishing Poles (or let each guest use their own)

A children's swimming pool filled with water

Wooden fish shapes (cut with a jig-saw), 1–3 per guest

Brass cup hooks

Black paint or permanent marker

Polyurethane or spray gloss finish, optional

What to do:

1. Before the party, paint or draw a black eye on one side of each fish. Write the word "PRIZE" on the back of a few. If you will be using these again after the party, coat them with a glossy finish to preserve them and to make them look nice. When dry, screw a cup hook into the center of each fish.

2. Before guests arrive, set up the pool and place the fish in the pond with the hooks facing up. Allow each child a turn at hooking a fish. Those who hook a fish with the word "PRIZE" on it win a prize. Un-hook the fish that have the word "PRIZE" written on them, and remove them from the pool, or shuffle them back in pool with the others to make it difficult to tell which ones are the "PRIZE" fish.

3. If desired, after the game is over, or at the end of the party, give each child a few fish to take home with their poles.

Variation: Use a stopwatch and give each child 15 or 30 seconds to catch as many fish as he can. Replace them for the others to catch afterwards. The one to catch the most fish wins.

Caution: Do not leave children unattended around the pool of water.

Go Fish

Purchase the card game Go Fish and play it. (It can also be played with regular cards.)

Spear Fishing

You will need:

A straight tree stick or a wooden dowel (if you have a toy Indian spear, that would be great)

A magnet (somewhat strong)

Tape, glue or string

Fish shapes cut from construction paper

A felt tip marker

A tub or small children's pool

Paper clips

What to do:

1. Before the party, attach the magnet to the stick with tape, glue or string.

2. Write on the back of one or two fish, "YOU WON!" and attach a paperclip to the other side of each fish.

3. Put the fish into the tub or pool, with the words facing down.

4. During the party, allow children to take turns sticking the stick into the tub and try to "spear" a fish, by letting the magnet touch the paperclip. The ones who get the fish that say "YOU WON!" win a prize. An appropriate prize would be a toy fish or a card game of "Go Fish."

Fish Tales

Everyone knows the old joke of "The Fish That Got Away." Maybe a friend you know or a relative tells tall tales of the fish that they catch. Isn't it amazing how a one-foot fish that someone has caught turns into a two-foot fish when they tell about their big catch?

Let the children sit in a circle and tell crazy, far-fetched fish stories. Start with the birthday child and then go clockwise.

Variation: If desired, have the birthday child begin the telling of the story and have the other children add on to it. Let the birthday child tell the ending.

Note: Remember to videotape this. It should be fun to listen to many years later.

☙ FAVOR AND ☙ PRIZE IDEAS

Goldfish shaped snack cracker bags, saltwater taffy, rolls of LifeSavers candy, fish bait (foam cups filled with gummy worms that have labels with the words "FISH BAIT" written on them), gummy fish, fishing hats (see Crafts), fish stickers, inexpensive plastic toy fish, hooked fish and Fishing Poles (see Crafts), inexpensive toy fishing poles, fishing lures (without hooks), toy boats, tub toys, Go Fish cards or real live goldfish with a jar of goldfish food (check with parents before the party to see how they feel about this).

Pool and Beach Party

Want to make a big splash with your guests? There's nothing like a pool or beach party to cool you off during the dog days of summer. Whether your guests swim or not they are sure to have a good time at this party. Most of the games are played outside of the pool, so that non-swimmers will feel very comfortable. Let the parents know this on the invitation. This is a party that will require much adult supervision. Read the helpful tips in this chapter to ensure smooth sailing for your pool or beach party. Now get ready for some fun in the sun!

🎉 SUNNY 🎉 INVITATION

Use bright yellow paper to make invitations as shown in the illustration (fig. 26a & b). For a beach party just change the word "pool" on the front of the invitation to "beach." When guests RSVP, find out whether they can swim. Explain to them that it is o.k. if they don't want to swim. Don't pressure them to swim. If this is a beach party, remind everyone to bring sandals.

🎉 DECORATIONS 🎉

If you will be holding your party at a beach, no decorations will be necessary. They may blow away. Otherwise:

- Decorate the mailbox, front porch, pool fence and lawn furniture with yellow, red and orange balloons and crepe paper.
- Put pinwheels in the ground near the front door or in pots near the pool area.

(a) (b)

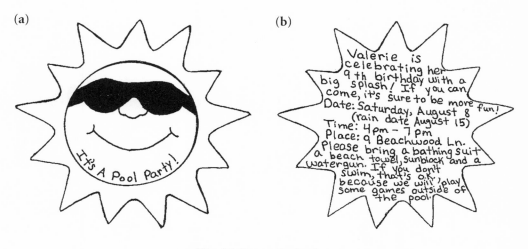

Fig. 26. Sunny Invitation

- Put a sign on your front door or gate instructing guests to come around to the backyard if necessary.

- Make a picture of a sun to hang on your front door or gate. Cut a circle out of yellow construction paper and glue red and orange triangles to it. If desired, give your sun a pair of black paper sunglasses and a big smiley face.

- Hang pictures of fish on a back door or window.

- Use yellow, red or orange tableware, or use tableware with fish designs. If you will be using a tablecloth and it's windy outside, hold it down with table clips, rocks or seashells.

- For a centerpiece, use dolls or action figures. Dress them in swimwear (e.g., bathing suits, scuba outfits, flippers, snorkels, etc.). Sit them in a pool of water.

- Play beach music such as "Itsy Bitsy Teeny Weeny Yellow Polka Dot Bikini," "Surfer Girl" (The Beach Boys), "Surfin'" (The Beach Boys), "Surfin' Safari" (The Beach Boys),

"Surfin' USA" (The Beach Boys), "Wipeout" (The Beach Boys), "Six Little Ducks"(for preschoolers — Joanie Bartels), "My Bonnie" (The Beatles), "Octopus's Garden" (The Beatles or Raffi), "Sailing" (NSYNC) or "Rock Lobster" (B52's).

🎉 FOOD 🎉

Beach Menu

If you will be taking your guests to the beach, keep everything in the cooler until serving time to prevent spoilage. Bring a large beach blanket for everyone to sit on, or let guests sit on their own. Bring a garbage bag for disposing of trash. Place each child's meal on a Frisbee lined with a paper napkin for a serving plate. After everyone has finished eating they can play with them. Write or paint the children's names on them before the party. You could even place their meals in a brand new personalized bucket.

- I Could Eat a Whale Sandwich: Cut bread with a fish shaped cookie cutter and spread peanut butter and jelly on it.
- Chips or goldfish shaped crackers
- Grapes
- Be sure to have plenty of canned drinks on hand (it will, most likely, be very hot)

Pool Menu

- Boat Sandwiches: Submarine sandwiches with a triangle paper or cheese sail stuck into each (skewer the sail with a shish-ka-bob skewer and discard skewer immediately after presenting).
- Celery Boats: fill celery stalks with peanut butter and stick a corn tortilla into the peanut butter as a sail
- Orange slices
- Blue Lagoon Drinks: Blue drinks with gummy fish ice cubes floating in them (fill ice cube trays with gummy fish, pour blue drink over them and freeze). Tell the children not to swallow the gummy fish.

Sunshine Cake

You will need:

1 box of cake mix, plus ingredients as box directs

5 cups yellow frosting

Two 1½-inch round chocolate peppermint patties

Black or red string licorice

What to do:

1. Using two 8- or 9-inch round pans, bake and cool cakes as di-
rected. Cut one of the cakes into 8 equal triangular sections, like a pie, as shown in diagram on next page (fig. 27a). Leave the remaining cake uncut; it will become the face of the sun.

2. Cut a round slice off the wide end of each triangle, as shown in diagram (fig. 27b). You can do this with the edge of the cake pan. Freeze all cake pieces, uncovered, for about 1 hour to make frosting spread more easily.

3. Remove from freezer and assemble on a foil-covered board as shown in diagram (fig. 27c).

4. Frost the entire cake yellow.

5. Place two chocolate peppermint patties on the circle as sunglasses. Use 3 pieces of string licorice for the sunglass frames. Use another piece of string licorice for the mouth and two short pieces for the corners of the mouth.

Beach Cake

You will need:

1 box cake mix, plus ingredients as box directs

4 cups white icing

Food coloring: tan and blue

Powdered sugar, optional

Gummy fish or fish shaped crackers

Fruit Roll-Ups, optional

Paper mix drink umbrella, optional

Gumballs, optional

Plastic people figures, optional

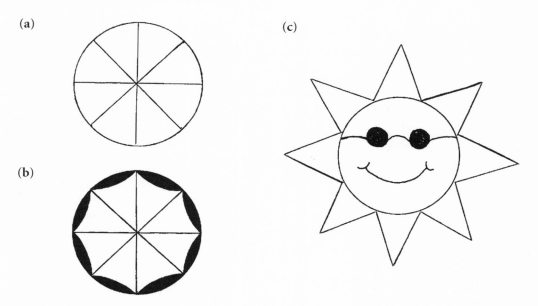

Fig. 27. Sunshine Cake

What to do:

1. Using a 9 × 13-inch pan, bake and cool cake as directed. Tint half of the frosting tan, and frost half of the cake tan to look like the sand of the beach. Tint the other half of the frosting blue, and frost the other half of the cake blue to look like water. Use a knife to lift up the icing and make waves. If desired, sprinkle with a little powdered sugar to make sea foam.

2. Press the gummy fish or fish shaped crackers into the "water."

3. Decorate the beach scene with plastic people figures. Cut a rectangle of Fruit Roll-Up to look like a beach towel by cutting fringes on the ends. Place a paper umbrella next to it as a beach umbrella. Use the gumballs as a beachballs.

Easy Fish Cupcakes

If time is short, bake a batch of cupcakes and frost them blue. Top them off with gummy fish.

Fish Cake

See Fishing Party.

🎉 HELPFUL TIPS 🎉

- Have plenty of adult or teen helpers around to help you keep a close eye on the children. Do not take your eye off children around water, even for a minute. If it makes you feel better, ask the parents to stay if they can.

- Have some extra beach towels on hand for those who forget to bring one.

- Have waterproof suntan lotion available for those who forget to bring some. Have at least 30 spf (skin protection factor) sunblock. Find a higher protection block if you can. Light skinned people burn very easily. Be absolutely sure that everyone is well covered with sunscreen. Don't forget spots like the feet, ears, the neck underneath the hair and underneath clothing. A T-shirt only provides an SPF factor of 5 or 7 when dry and virtually none when wet! Tell the younger children that you are rubbing on a magic force field and it should cause some giggles.

- Make sure that everyone wears sandals when walking on the sand. Beach sand can get hotter than 120°F and burn delicate tootsies!

- Bring a zippered sandwich bag stocked with bandages, wipes and a tube of antibiotic cream, just in case.

☙ CRAFTS ☙

Sun Visors

As children arrive, have them decorate inexpensive sunvisors (found at craft stores). You could even use sun hats or baseball caps. Put glue, plastic gems, beads and fabric paint on a table that is protected with newspaper. Let the children decorate as they please.

Sand Art Decorations

You will need:

Old food jars (baby food jars work great)
Colored sand (found at craft stores)
Disposable bowls
Plastic spoons
Glue
Masking tape

What to do:

1. Before the party, wash out the food jars and remove the labels. Label the bottom of each jar with a child's name using the masking tape.

2. During the party, you will need to set this craft up outdoors, since it is very messy. Put each color of sand in a different bowl with a plastic spoon stuck in each.

3. Let the children make one layer of each color in their jar.

4. Apply glue to the inside threads of the jar lid and screw the lid on tight. Tell the children that they can decorate their rooms with these, and remind them not to shake them.

Seashell Wind Chimes

If your children are anything like mine, then you probably have a bucket full of seashells hanging around your house from your last 10 trips to the seashore. This craft is a great way to get rid of them!

You will need:

1 clothes hanger per child
A bucket of sea shells (some will break when hammering)
Thin nails
A hammer
Fishing line
Nametags

What to do:

1. Before the party, make a hole in the top of each shell by lightly tapping the nail into it with the hammer. The holes should be wide enough for the fishing line to thread through.

2. Cut 5 lengths of string about 16 to 20 inches each.

3. String on one shell and knot it very tightly at the end of the fishing line.

4. Tie more shells down the same fishing line. Spread them about 2 inches apart. Knot the last shell about 4 inches from the top. Finish the other fishing lines the same as the first.

5. Tie the top of each string to the hanger. Tie a tight knot to secure. Place them evenly apart on the hanger. Tell the children to hang their wind chimes outdoors to catch the breeze. Place a nametag on each child's wind chimes.

🎉 GAMES AND 🎉 ACTIVITIES

Go to the Beach or Swim in a Pool

If you are lucky enough to live on or near the beach, let the children build sandcastles. If you have a sandbox, that would work well too. Play Frisbee, volleyball, badminton, horseshoes or lawn darts. Crank up the tunes and play some great beach music.

If you have a pool, belong to a swim club, or even have a small child's wading pool, let the children go swimming. If using a wading pool, fill it with some bubble bath suds and let the children play with the bubbles. You could even let them run through the sprinkler.

Many hotels and motels now rent out their pools for parties. Surprisingly, many high-end hotels do this. For many, it is a way to boost sales during slow seasons. Some have birthday party packages and are even equipped to hold a family reunion. You can go swimming at an indoor or outdoor pool, they will serve the food, cake, ice cream, decorations and more! They take care of everything. Some will even let the guests stay the night. My sister did this for my teenage niece's birthday, and the kids had a great time. What a great slumber party idea, and especially for those children with winter birthdays!

Caution: Do not leave children unattended near the pool.

Visit an Aquarium

Many cities, especially those near beaches, have large aquariums. If you live near one, call to see if they have group rates or birthday party activities. Many have touch exhibits that allow the children to actually touch the fish.

Water Paintings

Give each child a large-size old paintbrush. Set a bucket of water on your driveway, and encourage the children to dip their paintbrushes in the bucket, and "paint" pictures on your driveway.

Billowing Bubbles

Now here's a recipe for bubbles that you are going to like. It makes bubbles that really hang in there!

You will need:

A large jar

3 cups water

1 cup dishwashing detergent

6 Tbsp. light corn syrup

A large pan or bucket

Plastic six-pack packaging rings (uncut) from aluminum soda cans, preferably one per guest

1. Before the party, combine ingredients in a large jar or container, cover, and shake well. Let the mixture settle for a few hours.

2. During the party, pour the mixture into a large pan or bucket. Let the children dip their six-pack rings into the bubble mixture and wave them into the air!

Boat Race

You will need:

2 foam plates

2 shish-ka-bob skewers (with sharp points cut off)

2 triangular shaped sails

A small children's pool full of water

What to do:

1. Skewer the paper sails with your "mast."

2. Push the skewer into the center of the plate. You now have a boat ready to set sail!

3. Put the boats in the pool and line children up in two equal lines.

4. Two-by-two, let the children compete against one another, by blowing the boats across the pool. The child whose boat gets to the other side first wins.

Caution: Do not leave the children unattended near the pool and do not let them point the skewers at one another.

Note: If you like, let each child make his own boat for the race.

Water Balloon Toss

Now what would a summer pool party be without this game? It's great for cooling kids off on a hot summer day!

You will need:

Balloons filled with water and tied closed, 1 for every 2 guests

A bucket or tub to hold the balloons in

String or garden hose, for a line marker

A whistle

What to do:

1. Lay the string or garden hose out in a straight long line.

2. Tell the children to choose a partner. If someone does not have a partner, I'm sure a sweltering hot adult will be willing to fill in.

3. Tell the children to stand on the string, across from their partners. Their partners should

be about 3 feet away from them.

4. Have an adult pass out one balloon to each pair of partners standing on the line.

5. At the blow of the whistle the children gently toss their balloons to their partners on the other side of the line. Do not let the partners toss them immediately back! They need to stop after the first toss. Any two team members to drop their balloon and break it are out of the game.

6. After the first toss, the children must each take one step back. Check to make sure that everyone is evenly back from the marked line. Remind them to wait to toss the balloon until they hear the sound of the whistle.

7. Blow the whistle, and then the partners all toss the balloons back. They continue passing and stepping back in this manner until only two team members are left. They can be declared the winning team members, or they may continue passing the balloon to one another until the balloon breaks.

Fill the Bucket Relay

You will need:

2 plastic cups
2 medium size pails or buckets of equal size filled with water (household pails work well)
2 small empty pails or buckets of equal size (beach pails work well)

What to do:

1. Divide the children into two equal teams and line them up behind a marked line.

2. Place one bucket full of water in front of each line of team members and place the empty buckets about 20 feet away.

3. Hand a cup to the first child in each line. Tell them that they are to fill their cups up with water by scooping up some water from the bucket in front of them.

4. At the signal to go, they must run or walk as fast as they can to their team's empty bucket and pour the water into it. Remind them not to spill it. If they do they must run back and refill their cup.

5. When they have emptied their cups they must run back and pass the empty cups to the next team members in line, who then do the same as the first two children. This continues until the empty bucket is full and the full bucket is empty. The first team to overflow their smaller bucket wins.

Crab Walk Relay

You will need:

A whistle

What to do:

1. Divide the children into two equal teams and line them up behind a start line. Set another goal line about 20 feet away. If

you will be playing this game on the beach, goal lines can be scratched into the sand with a stick.

2. Have the first two children in each line get down on the ground and put their hands behind their backs. Their feet should be facing toward their team members.

3. At the signal to go (the blow of a whistle), they must race backwards on all fours to the goal.

4. As soon as the first team member reaches the goal, the next child in line must do the same as the first child. Watch for cheaters. No one may go until the child before him reaches the goal. As soon as the second child reaches the goal, the next child goes, and so on. The first team to have all of its players finish wins.

Sand Treasure Hunt

You will need:

A sandbox, sand filled pool or large tub

Inexpensive toys (e.g., rubber balls, plastic animals, toy cars, toy boats, plastic gold coins, seashells, etc.)

Shovels and pails

Acrylic paint, optional

What to do:

1. Before the party, paint the children's names onto the pails.

2. The day of the party, hide all of the "treasure" in the sandbox (not too deep).

3. During the party, hand each child a shovel and pail. Tell them to dig for the buried treasure and to place it in their pails.

Balloon Race

You will need:

One inflated balloon for each guest

A whistle

A large swimming pool

What to do:

1. Line all of the guests up along one side of the pool, with their balloons in front of them, on the water. Place any inexperienced swimmers at the shallow end of the pool.

2. At the blow of the whistle, they are to knock their balloon to the other side of the pool as they swim. The first one to the other side of the pool wins.

Caution: Do not leave the children unattended near the water.

Marco Polo

You will need:

A large swimming pool

What to do:

1. All of the children get into the pool (shallow end only, unless you have all experienced swimmers). Choose one child to be "It."

2. "It" closes his eyes and counts to 10, while all of the other children spread out.

3. Once "It" reaches 10 he calls out "Marco," with his eyes closed.

4. The others then respond by yelling "Polo."

5. "It" must try to tag one of the other players, by listening to their voices. The child who gets tagged becomes the next "It."

Caution: Do not leave the children unattended near the water.

Make a Wish Penny Toss

You will need:

A small swimming pool or tub filled with water

Two or three plastic lids (e.g., margarine, coffee, cream cheese, etc.)

Three pennies for each child

What to do:

1. Place the lids into the pool or tub and line the children up a few feet back.

2. Give each child three pennies to try and toss onto the floating lids. If he lands one on a lid, he makes a wish and wins a prize!

Caution: Do not leave the children unattended near the water.

Variation: Allow the children to jump into the pool for the pennies after the game. The one to get the most wins a prize. Let those who can't swim help you toss more pennies into the pool. Just make sure that no one is in the way when the pennies are tossed. Award prizes to helpers.

Sponge Tag

You will need:

A large, clean, soft sponge (the type used to wash cars)

A bucket of water

What to do:

Choose one child to be "It." Soak the sponge in the bucket of water. "It" must then throw the sponge at the other children. The child tagged becomes the next "It."

Squirt the Balloon

You will need:

A rope or clothesline

Clothespins

A lot of inflated balloons

A string or a hose for a marker

A water gun

What to do:

1. Suspend the rope or clothesline between two trees or poles, and hang the inflated balloons from it with the clothespins.

2. Line the children up behind the marked line and let them take turns at trying to shoot a balloon. Anyone hitting one wins.

Note: If it is windy outside, this game will be difficult to play. To make this game more challenging do not use a powerful water gun.

Variation: Use lightweight plastic balls to hit the balloons.

Sand-Sculpting Contest

If your party will be held at the beach, this is a good activity to keep everyone quite busy. Divide the children into two or more groups and see who can create the most unique sculpture. Moms and dads may want to join a team and really get competitive. Use seaweed for hair and clothing. Use shells for eyes, claws and teeth. Remember to get a picture of everyone in front of their masterpieces.

Pool Basketball

Play as you would regular basketball, but use a beachball instead of a basketball. For goals use garbage cans, tubs or baskets.

Seashell Hunt

Hide seashells around your house. Hand each child a personalized beach pail. At the blow of a whistle, send them to find the seashells. The child to find the most wins.

Shaking the Coconut Tree

See the Barnyard Party game "Shaking the Apple Tree." Replace the word "apple" with "coconut."

Man Overboard

See Fishing Party.

Fish Guess

See Fishing Party.

Hook the Fish

See Fishing Party.

Pop Up

See Sports Party. Use a beachball for this game.

🎉 FAVOR AND 🎉 PRIZE IDEAS

Pinwheels, plastic beach pails and shovels, bottles of blowing bubbles, sunglasses, squirt guns, sand sifters, sidewalk chalk, snorkels, swim goggles, jump-ropes, balls, beachballs, flying discs, sailboats, suntan lotion, decorative seashells, sand dollars, dried starfish, captain or sailor hats, gummy shark candy, marine animal crackers, saltwater taffy, kites for beach parties, Sun Visors (see Crafts), Sand Art Decorations (see Crafts) or Seashell Wind Chimes (see Crafts).

Sports Party

Hey sports fans, do you want to have a party with lots of heart-pumping action? Well, this is a party that's sure to be a slam-dunk with any guest! If your little sports fan has his heart set on a sports themed birthday party, don't let the fact that you have a small yard hold you back. Take everyone to a playing field. Read on for more information in this chapter. Now get your running shoes ready, because you're going to have a ball!

SPORTS BALL INVITATION

Invitations with sports themes on them are easy to find at stores, but if you prefer to make your own see illustrations (28a & b, 29, 30 and 31) for some ideas. Use white paper circles for the baseball invitation, and use red ink for the stitches. For a soccer ball invitation, draw colorful hexagon or pentagon shapes onto a white paper circle. Use orange paper for basketballs and footballs, and draw on black seams and stitches. Write your message on the back of the paper. Ask guests on the invitation to bring a baseball mitt, if necessary. Suggest that guests come dressed in their favorite sports outfit, or ask half of the guests to come dressed in red and the other half blue. The colors would help to determine who belongs on what team during the party. Just make sure that you divide the groups up equally according to athletic ability. Your child would be the best person to know the placement of team members.

DECORATIONS

- Decorate the mailbox, front porch and party area with balloons and streamers in the color of your child's favorite team.
- Cut a large ball out of construction paper or posterboard and hang it on the front door.

(a)

(b)

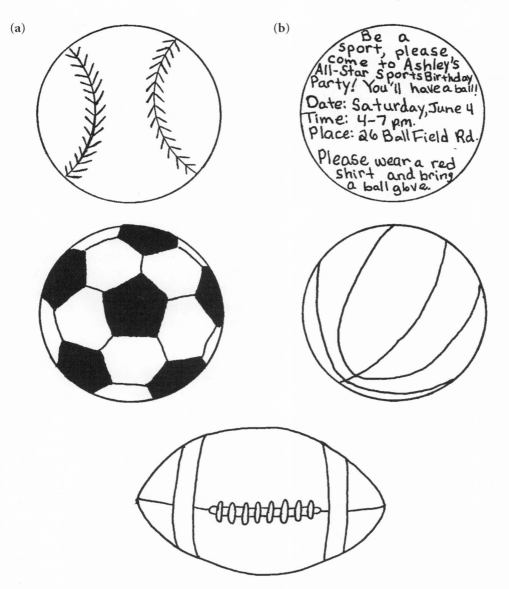

Be a sport, please come to Ashley's All-Star Sports Birthday Party! You'll have a ball!
Date: Saturday, June 4
Time: 4-7 pm.
Place: 26 Ball Field Rd.

Please wear a red shirt and bring a ball glove.

Top row: Fig. 28(a and b). Baseball invitation. Middle row,

- Hang pennants or posters of your child's favorite team or players.
- Cut out sports balls from construction paper, or print on your computer, and hang in the party area.
- If the party will be held at a local ball field, hang streamers and balloons

from a fence, benches or a picnic pavilion. Just be sure to clean it all up before you leave.

- Purchase inexpensive plastic trophies and paint the children's names on them. Use them as place cards.
- Use tableware with sports balls on it,

or use a green tablecloth and tape paper ball shapes onto it. You could even decorate the table to look like a football field by taping white crepe paper onto the green tablecloth as yard lines. Use white tape or white paper to write the numbers.

- For the centerpiece, use a sports ball, football helmet, a baseball mitt, pompoms, megaphones, or even a trophy that your child is very proud of.

- Play songs like "Baseball on the Block" (John McCutcheon), "Take Me Out to the Ballgame" (Raffi), "We Are the Champions" (Queen) or "Star Spangled Banner."

♟ FOOD ♟

If you are holding your party at an athletic field and it has a grill, cook out there. If not, pack sandwiches. Someone with a good sense of humor could play a concessionaire by wearing a serving box (a cardboard box with a rope tied to it) and walking around at serving time with the food. This person can yell "Peanuts! Popcorn! Get your hot fresh popcorn!" or "Get your ice cold drinks!" Place the popcorn in paper bags or use popcorn boxes purchased at party supply stores. Purchase peanuts in individual bags.

- Hot dogs and condiments (what would a trip to the ballgame be without them?)

- One or two of the following: Chips, popcorn, peanuts, nachos or hot baked pretzels

- Cantaloupe melon balls

- Root beer or Gatorade sports drink

Soccer Ball Cake

Frost the sides of a round layer cake white. Make a hexagon shaped template out of cardboard, and lightly trace the shapes onto the cake with a knife. These cuts are a visual guide for your colored hexagon shapes. Look at a real soccer ball for a visual guide. Using a star tip, frost the center hexagon with colored frosting (e.g., red, blue, green, etc.). Frost the surrounding hexagons white. The hexagons around the edge of the cake should alternate white and colored. Use the colored frosting to border all of the white hexagons.

Baseball Cake

Frost a round layer cake white. Use red or black string licorice for the stitches.

Football Field Cake

You will need:

1 box of cake mix, plus ingredients as box directs

3 cups green frosting

½–1 cup white frosting

6 bendable straws

Scissors

Plastic football player figures, optional (purchase at a craft store)

A chocolate foil covered football (purchased at a candy store)

What to do:

1. Using a 9 × 13-inch pan, bake and cool the cake as directed. Freeze, uncovered, for about an hour to make frosting spread easier.

2. Frost the entire cake green.

3. Using a decorator's bag and a small round tip, frost white yard lines across the cake.

4. Take three bendable straws and bend two of them. Cut two slits near the top of the third straw, one on each side, using a sharp knife. Using the scissors, cut off enough of the ends of the other two straws to resemble a goal post when stuck into the slits (see fig. 32). Make another goal post like the first. Push one into each end of the cake.

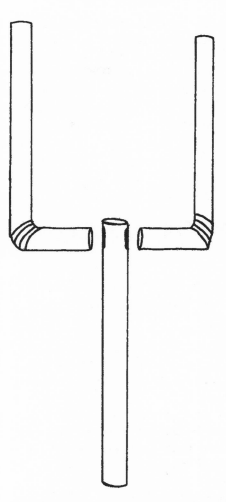

Fig. 32. Goal Post for Football Cake

⛳ CRAFTS ⛳

Decorated Caps

You will need:

Plain baseball caps (with no logos)
Fabric paint or felt tip marker
Sport ball pins and/or craft jewels
Glue, for jewels
Newspaper or paper tablecloth

What to do:

1. Cover a table with newspaper or tablecloth. Set all of the items out on top of the table.

2. As guests arrive, let them decorate the caps with pins or jew-els. Put their names on the caps with paints or markers.

🎉 GAMES AND 🎉 ACTIVITIES

Let's Plaaay Ball!!!

Choose your child's favorite sport and have a ball game. Use tennis balls to play baseball with; they are a lot safer and just as fun. If your yard isn't large enough to play sports games, consider having the party at an athletic field. Some city parks and recreation facilities will rent out their fields and reserve their picnic areas for you. Call them well in advance. Check to see if there is a restroom nearby that will be available. If not, make sure that everyone goes to the restroom before leaving for the field. Bring plenty of drinks, because everyone is going to get thirsty. Bring a first aid kit … just in case.

Take Me Out to the Ballgame

Consider taking the children to a local ball game. If any of your child's friends are not as crazy about sports as your child is, this of course would not be fun for them. Find out before planning this outing. If the weather permits, you could have a tailgate party, or you could bring the guests back to your home for cake and ice cream.

Three Cheers for the Birthday Kid!

Let the children create team cheers or do ones that they are familiar with. Have the guests make up a silly birthday cheer for the birthday child. They could show off some cheerleading or dance moves that they know.

Star Athlete Guess

Have your child find out before the party if your guests are into sports. If they don't know anything about famous athletes this game would not go

over well. If you know all of your child's friends are also sports fanatics, then go for it, and realize that you may have a lot of winners on this game!

You will need:

> Pictures of famous athletes from sports magazines or from the newspaper
> Yellow construction paper
> Glue
> Pen or felt tip marker
> Paper, 1 sheet per guest
> Pencils, 1 per guest

What to do:

1. Before the party, cut star shapes out of the yellow paper. Glue each athlete's picture to a star and number the star with a pen or marker.

2. During the party, set the pictures out on a table. As the guests arrive, hand them a pencil and a piece of paper. Have them write down the athlete's name that they guess corresponds with each number on the picture. The one to guess the most correctly wins. An appropriate prize would be a pack of baseball cards.

Dizzy Bat Race

You will need:

> 2 baseball bats
> A whistle

What to do:

1. Divide the children into two teams and stand them behind a starting line.

2. Approximately 20–30 feet away, lay two baseball bats on the ground.

3. At the blow of a whistle, the first child in each line must run to his team's bat, put the handle end of the bat to his forehead, put the other end to the ground and spin (running) around the bat 3 times. The end of the bat must stay on the ground. Watch for cheaters.

4. He then runs back to his team and touches off with the next child in line, who then does the same. This continues on until one team has all of its members finish first. They are declared the winning team.

Note: It would be best to play this game on grass, just in case someone gets so dizzy that they fall.

Pop Up

A tennis ball
Baseball mitts, optional
Nametags (if some of the children do not know one another)

What to do:

1. Have the players form a circle, and choose one child to go in the center.

2. The child in the center tosses the ball high while calling out the name of a child in the circle.

3. The player whose name was called must catch the ball before it bounces more than once. If the player catches the ball, that player changes places with the child in the center and becomes the next ball-tosser. If the ball is not caught, the first ball-tosser continues to toss the ball and call out names until a player is successful in catching the ball. If time allows, play until everyone has had a turn.

Hoop Toss

You will need:

A hula-hoop
2 ropes
2 trees or poles
A football, baseball or tennis ball

What to do:

1. Tie the hula-hoop between two trees or poles, at the average guest's eye level.

2. Line the children up and have them take turns trying to throw the ball through the hoop. Anyone to get the ball through wins a prize.

Variation: If desired, have all three different types of balls or three of one type of ball. Give the children three shots. The one to get the most through the hoop wins a prize.

Obstacle Course

Make an obstacle course of several sports feats. How many of the following obstacles that you use will all depend on the size of the yard that you have, or the size of the area you will be playing in. Pick the obstacles that best suit the circumstances. Arrange them in any order that you choose. Keep the children's ages in mind when planning the obstacle course. Don't plan too many feats for small children. Time the children with a stopwatch or a watch with a second hand. Set up start and finish points and mark them with signs. You will also need to post the instructions on large pieces of cardboard so the guests will know what to do as they move along the track. It will be too hard to remember the steps. It would also be a good idea to have someone show them what to do before beginning the game. Some children may not know what an obstacle course is.

- Slalom course: Set up boxes or sport cones in a zigzag manner and set a soccer ball in front of them. Have the children kick the soccer ball around the boxes or cones.
- Jump rope 5–20 times (depending on the age group).
- Dribble a basketball to a hoop and shoot a basket (the ball must go into the basket).
- Throw a ball through a hanging hula-hoop.
- Hula-hoop treading: set 4–6 hula-hoops on the ground, two by two. Have the children try to run through them, stepping into the left-side hoop with the left foot, the right-side hoop with the right, and so on. Borrow hula-hoops from friends or purchase one for each guest to take home after the party. For parties with teenagers, use old tires or spare tires instead of hula-hoops.
- Do 10 jumping jacks.
- Lawn chair crawl: Set up a row of lawn chairs so that the children can crawl underneath them.

Golf Course

You will need:

A golf set (adult's or children's)

Plastic golf balls

4–9 plastic disposable cups or aluminum vegetable cans (if using cans file any sharp edges down)

Paint

Pencil and paper for keeping score

What to do:

1. Before the party, paint numbers on the cups or cans, and allow to dry.

2. During the party, lay the cups or cans in the yard (or at an athletic field) as a pretend golf course.

3. The children must "tee off" 5–10 feet (depending on the age) away from cup #1. Just like real golf, they must try to get the ball into the cup or can with the fewest strokes. Once it is hit in, write down the number of strokes they took to get it in.

4. The child then must take the ball out of the cup, place the ball next to cup #1, and see how many strokes it takes to get the ball in each of the remaining cups. The children go to the cups in numerical order. The child finishing with the fewest total strokes wins.

Note: If desired, have more than one child play at a time to speed things up, or use fewer cups.

Catch the Ball

See Pool and Beach Party game "Water Balloon Toss." This game is played just like the Water Balloon Toss game. The only difference between the two is that each player will need a baseball mitt, and instead of playing the game with water balloons, it is played with tennis balls. (And of course, the tennis ball won't pop!) A team is "out" when one partner drops the ball. You will need one ball for every two players.

Thumb Wrestling

1, 2, 3, 4, let's start the thumb war!

What to do:

1. Two players sit facing each other, and hook the fingers of their right hands together so that both of their right thumbs are sticking straight up.

2. As they say, "1, 2, 3, 4, I declare thumb war!" they move their thumbs from side to side with each word spoken.

3. Once the word "war" is reached, each child must try to pin down the opponent's right thumb using his right thumb.

The first one to pin down his opponent's thumb wins.

Note: If awarding prizes, have only two opponents go at one time, so that you may watch for the winner. Have everyone watch and be the audience. If desired, have all of the winners play against one another until you are down to only two winners who then compete against one another.

🎉 FAVOR AND 🎉 PRIZE IDEAS

Look for items with sports balls or team logos on them (e.g., pens, pencils, erasers, pennants, notepads, stickers, keychains), baseballs, baseball holders, sports trading cards (the kind with bubble gum in the pack), baseball shaped gumballs, foil-wrapped sport ball candy, plastic trophies, whistles, Baby Ruth candy bars, Big League Chew shredded bubble gum, inexpensive mini basketball sets or baseball caps (see Crafts).

Note: If the invited guests are all good friends of one another, let them autograph one another's baseballs.

Race Car Party

Rev your engines and get ready for life in the fun lane with this party! Your little race car fanatic will have fun pretending that he and his friends are members of a pit crew, or race car drivers speeding down the track. The light is green, hold on and have fun ... you're goin' racin'!

of the paper, and put your message on the back. You could even make a stop sign, stoplight or checkered flag invitation. If you have a computer, print a race car invitation using the wording illustrated.

🎉 RACE CAR 🎉 INVITATION

Make an invitation like the one illustrated (fig. 33) using brightly colored construction paper (make the tires black). Make your designs on the front

🎉 DECORATIONS 🎉

- Decide on a color scheme for your decorations. You could use red, yellow and green (to resemble a stoplight), or black, white and red (to represent the checkered flag). Use the colors for hanging balloons and crepe paper streamers from your mailbox, front porch, fence or party area.

(a)

(b)

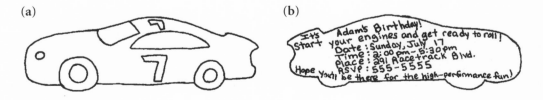

Fig. 33. Race Car Invitation

126

- Place a picture of a race car on your front door or gate. Above the picture write something like, "Welcome to Jonathan's race car party!" and underneath write, "Race on in!" You could even make a sign and write "Erica's Grand Prix," "Zack's Motor Speedway" or "Party Zone."

- Put a sign in the kitchen or where the refreshments will be served that reads, "Pit Stop" or "Filling Station."

- Put signs around the house that read "No Parking," "Speed Limit 5 MPH," "Kid Zone" or "Birthday Zone." Put one next to the driveway that reads, "Passenger unloading."

- Make pictures of stoplights. Cut rectangles out of black construction paper and glue red, yellow and green circles to them.

- Hang black and white checkered flags in the party room. These can be found at party supply stores.

- Put spare tires from your car in the yard, preferably the backyard. Use them for the game Pit Crew.

- Rent a police uniform and have an adult wear it, or have a friend who is a police officer come dressed in uniform. Give pretend tickets out to children for speeding, but joke about it and make them laugh.

- Play songs like "Drive My Car" (The Beatles), "Drive My Car" (Elmo — for preschoolers), "On the Road to Where We're Going" (Joanie Bartels — for preschoolers), "This Old Car" (Pete Seeger), "Electric Avenue" (Eddy Grant), "Car Wash" (Rose Royce), "Freeway of Love" (Aretha Franklin), "Every Day Is a Winding Road" (Sheryl Crow), "Little Deuce Coupe" (The Beach Boys), "Beep Beep" (The Playmates) or "Born to Be Wild" (Steppenwolf).

🎉 FOOD 🎉

Let the children pretend that they are at a drive-in or drive-through restaurant. Let them pretend to drive their car up to a window to get their order, or someone could deliver their meal to them on roller-skates, like at a drive-in.

- Cut bread slices with a car-shaped cookie cutter and top with peanut butter and jelly. You could even serve hamburger or hot dog "kid meals" in decorated paper bags.

- Individual bags of chips.

- Small apples or individual boxes of raisins.

- Complete the "kid meals" with a party favor in the bag as a surprise, just like at a restaurant.

Racetrack Cake

You will need:

> 1 box of cake mix, plus ingredients as box directs
>
> Green icing
>
> Brown or chocolate icing
>
> White candies such as white Good & Plenty, or use cut white marshmallow slivers
>
> Oreo or other chocolate sandwich cookies, optional
>
> A small toy race car

What to do:

1. Using a 9 × 13-inch pan, bake and cool cake as directed. Frost on a narrow brown strip across the sheetcake, lengthwise, to resemble the racetrack or road.

2. Use white candies for the lines down the center of the road.

3. Frost the rest of the cake green, using a frosting bag with a star tip, to resemble grass.

4. Cut the sandwich cookies in half and stick them in the cake edges to resemble old tires, as a guardrail.

5. Place the toy car on the road.

Race Car Cake

You will need:

1 box cake mix, plus ingredients as box directs

1 cup red or blue frosting

¾ cup yellow frosting

2 cups green frosting

1½-inch round chocolate peppermint patties

2 small round yellow candies, such as M & M's or gumdrops

3 1½-inch pieces of red or black string licorice

What to do:

1. Using a 9 × 13-inch pan, bake and cool cake as directed. Use a sharp knife to trace your car outline (see fig. 34), being careful not to cut too deep. This should be only a shallow cut for a visual aid when frosting. Trace the top of the car and the windows.

2. Frost the car body red or blue with a frosting bag and a star tip.

3. Frost the windows yellow with a frosting bag and a star tip.

4. Mix any remaining blue or yellow frosting together to add with the green frosting (blue and yellow make green). Frost the background and the sides of the cake green to resemble grass.

5. Put the peppermint patties on as wheels.

6. Put the yellow candies on as headlights.

7. Put the licorice on as the car radiator grills.

Fig. 34. Race Car Cake

🎉 CRAFTS 🎉

Racetrack Mats

You will need:

1 large piece of posterboard or cardboard per guest

A pad of construction paper with various colors

Safety scissors

Glue

Felt tip markers

Toy cars

What to do:

1. During the party, lay out all of the materials on a floor or ground and let the children cut out roads, houses, driveways, trees, people, animals, etc.

2. Have them glue the paper shapes onto the posterboard or cardboard and allow it to dry. After these have dried, the children can play with their toy cars on their pretend roads.

🎉 GAMES AND 🎉 ACTIVITIES

Driver's Test

If you have a battery-operated children's riding car, or a remote control car, let the children take turns playing with it. If necessary, set a timer for one or two minutes per turn. Make sure that you have extra batteries, or charge rechargeable batteries the day before the party. If you have field sports pylon cones, set them up so that the children can weave the cars in and out of the cones for fun. If you don't have sports pylon cones, use boxes and decorate them to look like houses or buildings.

Vroom Vroom!

After the Racetrack Mats have dried, let the children play with their cars on them. If you don't make the mats, then supply the children with some city building materials: blocks, boxes, toy houses, small people figures, etc. Let them make roads out of yarn. Get in on the action, and give them a few ideas — you're never too old to get down on the floor and play cars! Dads may enjoy doing this while Mom prepares lunch, or vice-versa.

Let's Go to the Races

Consider taking a small group of children to your local motor speedway or racetrack. Drivers occasionally do public appearances for their sponsors and sign autographs during special events. Some motor speedways have events for children with fun and games. The children would enjoy going on these days. Some cities have smaller tracks that are less expensive than the larger tracks and may even be just as fun, if not more fun.

See How Cars Are Made

Another trip that you might consider is to take the children to an automotive plant or factory if you live near one. I still have great memories of the trips that I took as a child to the Ford Motor plants in Detroit, Michigan. To a child, that is pretty impressive. Call well in advance to set up a tour.

Take a Trip to a Go-Cart Track

If you have a fun park near your home with go-carts that the children can ride, consider meeting everyone there. After everyone has had a turn or two on the track, or even a race car simulator, take everyone back to your home for some games, cake and ice cream.

Guess the Make

This is an activity for older children who are just beginning to recognize cars that they like.

You will need:

Pictures of cars from magazines

Sheets of construction paper, 1 per car picture

Glue

Felt tip markers

Paper, 1 sheet per guest

Pencils, 1 per guest

What to do:

1. Before the party, glue one picture to each sheet of paper and use markers to write a number on the sheet. If necessary, write the name of the car on the back of the paper or on a separate sheet of paper to help you remember them.

2. During the party, pass out the paper and pencils and tell guests to number their papers. Tell the guests to write down what they guess is the make of each car. The one to guess the most correctly wins.

Race Car Relay

If you only have one children's battery-operated car or pedal car for this game, ask a friend or guest if they could bring one. The two cars must be equal in their performance, though. Be

sure to charge them the day before the party to assure equal performance. You will need to show any children who are unfamiliar with the type of car you have chosen how to ride it before the game.

You will need:

2 battery-operated riding cars or pedal cars

2 chairs

2 bike horns

A checkered flag, optional

What to do:

1. Divide the children into two equal teams and line them up behind a marked start line. The first two children in line get into or onto their cars. Remind them not to go until they see the flag wave.

2. Place the two chairs about 20–30 feet away from the start line. The distance that you set them away from the start line will depend on the length of your driveway and the area that you have chosen. (Play only in a safe area where there are no moving vehicles.) Place one horn on each chair.

3. At the wave of the checkered flag, the children with the cars race to the chairs, honk the horns, put them back down, race back to the starting line and get out of the cars.

4. The next child in each line then gets into the car and does the same. This continues until one team has all of its players finish. That is the winning

team. As they win, wave the checkered flag again. An appropriate prize would be a plastic toy trophy cup for each child on the winning team. If you have very young children, which you most likely will for this game, award every child a prize.

Hunt for Hidden Cars or Tools

If your house is anything like my house, it seems like whenever you need a tool it is missing from its usual place, or you are constantly finding toy cars in odd places. Here is a game where they are hidden on purpose. Hide several toy cars or tools (not too sharp or pointy) around your house and send the children looking for them. (They may just find one that you have been looking for and wasn't intentionally hidden!) The one that finds the most wins a prize. An appropriate prize might be a toy car or a tape measure.

Name the Parts

Hand each child a piece of paper and a pencil, and tell them to write down as many parts to a car as they can think of. Some examples are as follows:

1. Door	10. Glove compartment
2. Hood	11. Bumper
3. Seat	12. Headlight
4. Wheel	13. Radio
5. Hub	14. Windshield wiper
6. Radiator	15. Mirror
7. Windshield	16. Gas pedal
8. Steering wheel	17. Speedometer
9. Seatbelt	18. Gas tank

The one to name the most parts wins.

Tire Blow Out

This is a very noisy game, but the children love it! Get your earplugs ready!

You will need:

1 inflated balloon per child, plus a few extra (if desired, half one color, half another)

2 laundry baskets

2 chairs

What to do:

1. Before the party, inflate all of the balloons. Put half of the balloons in one basket and the other half in the other basket. There should be an equal number in each basket. If using two different colors, put one color in one basket and the other color in the other basket.

2. During the party, divide the children into two equal teams, and line them up single file behind a marked line.

3. Place the two chairs 20–30 feet away from the starting point and facing the children. Put one laundry basket full of balloons behind each chair.

4. At the signal to go, the first child in each line runs to his team's chair, grabs a balloon from behind the chair, sits on the balloon, pops it, returns to his team and touches off the next child in line.

5. The next child in line does the same. This continues until one team has all of its members finish. They are declared the winning team.

Downhill Racers

2 boards of wood or cardboard 5–8 feet long

4 strips of wood 5–8 feet long, if using the wood for a ramp

Hammer and nails, if using wood

Something to prop a ramp up on: a picnic table, the back of a chair, the back of an open truck bed, etc.

One toy car per guest

A whistle

What to do:

1. Assemble two ramps before the party. You will need to create walls on the sides of the ramp to keep the cars from falling off. If using wood, nail a wood strip to each outside edge of each board. If using cardboard, just bend the sides of the cardboard up.

2. During the party, let children compete against one another by racing their toy cars down the ramps. Two children will race on each turn. At the blow of the whistle, the two competing let go of their cars. The first one down wins. An appropriate prize for each winning child might be a plastic inexpensive trophy. Another prize idea might be play money or a pretend check for an outrageous amount of money. All children get to keep their racecars. After the party, keep these racing ramps. Your child and his friends will have fun reusing them!

Pit Crew

You will need:

A spare tire from a car

A pair of gloves, preferably children's garden gloves (found at hardware stores)

A whistle

A stopwatch or a watch second hand

Pencil and paper for keeping score

What to do:

1. Set up a marked start line, and a finish line about 20–30 feet away.

2. Line the children up behind the start line and place a spare tire on the start line.

3. The first child in line puts on the gloves. At the blow of the whistle, he must roll the spare tire to the finish line as fast as he can. At the moment that the whistle is blown, start the time on the stopwatch. When he reaches the finish line, stop the timer and record the time that it took for him to reach it. The child with the fastest time wins.

Variation: If the children are big enough, and time allows, make the race more challenging by having the children turn the tire around at the finish line and return with it.

Filling the Radiator Relay

See Pool and Beach Party game "Fill the Bucket Relay."

Red Light, Green Light

Mark a start and finish line. Choose one child to be "It" and have him stand at the finish line with his back to the other children, who all line up along the start line. Have It begin counting aloud. As soon as he starts to count, the other children should begin running toward him. At any time It may shout, "Red light!" and turn around. The other children must immediately freeze. Anyone who keeps moving must return to the starting line. It then turns back around, yells, "Green light!" and begins counting again. The children run forward as before. The game continues in this manner until one child reaches It and tags him, becoming the new It.

☝ FAVOR AND ☝ PRIZE IDEAS

Toy cars, small tools, books or magazines about cars, checkered flags, car stickers, car erasers, posters of cars, school folders with race cars on them, car trip games and activity pads, road maps of different states, race car driver trading cards, plastic toy trophy cups or play money.

Fire Engine Party

Just look at any child's face as a big red firetruck flashes by, and you'll soon realize that most children are excited by the presence of a firetruck. Maybe it's the look and sound of it that excites them, but I suppose that we also view firefighters as heroes and children pick up on that. What perfect role models for our children — they are real, not some cartoon characters. Read on to see how to put on a sizzling good party!

🎉 FIRE ENGINE 🎉 INVITATION

Make an invitation in the shape of a firefighter hat, or try a fire engine as illustrated (fig. 35) using red construction paper. Use yellow paper for a rectangular window and 3 black paper circles for the wheels.

🎉 DECORATIONS 🎉

- Decorate the mailbox, front porch, fence and party area with red, yellow, white and black balloons and crepe paper.

- Put a picture of a fire engine on the front door. Make it out of red construction paper. Make black paper circles for wheels and a black ladder. Cut a yellow rectangle for the window. Underneath it write something like, "Happy Birthday, Firechief Michael."

- Decorate the table with a red tablecloth. Use yellow and black plates, cups and napkins. Some party supply stores may carry tableware with a firetruck theme. You could even use dalmatian dog tableware.

- For a table centerpiece, place a toy firetruck, firefighter hat, or even a stuffed dalmatian.

- Make pictures of fire engines, fire hydrants, dalmatians and firefighter hats out of construction paper or

(a) (b)

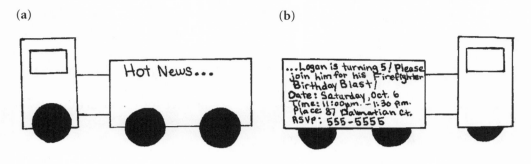

Fig. 35. Fire Engine Invitation

print on a computer printer and hang in the party area.

- Paint a large appliance box to resemble a firetruck. Paint it red, and paint on a black ladder and wheels. Use two aluminum pie plates for headlights, or cut them from yellow construction paper. Cut holes for the windows with a craft knife.

- Play songs like "Great Balls of Fire" (Jerry Lee Lewis) or "The Roof Is on Fire" (various artists).

☙ FOOD ☙

- Fire Engine Sandwich: peanut butter and jelly sandwiches cut with a firetruck shaped cookie cutter, or just cut as illustrated (fig. 36). Use black or red licorice for the ladder and chocolate cookies for the wheels (chocolate wafers or fudge topped cookies work well).

- Small apples, peaches or pears

- Potato chips

- Kool Aid in red cups

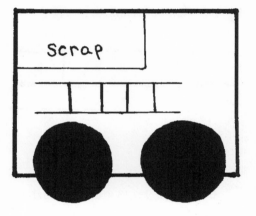

Fig. 36. Fire Engine Sandwich

Fire Engine Cake

You will need:

1 box cake mix, plus ingredients as box directs

5½ cups red frosting

½ cup yellow frosting

Assorted candies: 2 yellow gumdrops, 2 white Chiclets gum, black string licorice, black rope licorice and 6 1½-inch round chocolate peppermint patties (or 6 chocolate sandwich cookies).

(a — top view of cake; cut as shown)

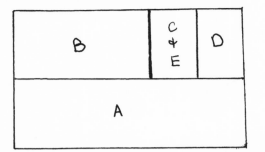

(b — side view of assembled pieces)

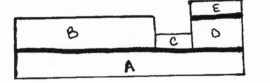

chocolate cookies onto the sides of the cake as wheels.

5. For the ladder, put strips of string licorice across the back of the truck and use rope licorice for the sides of the ladder.

(c — finished cake)

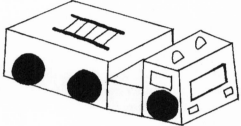

Fig. 37. Fire Engine Cake

What to do:

1. Using a 9 × 13-inch pan, bake and cool cake as directed. Cut as illustrated (fig. 37a) and freeze uncovered for at least one hour so that frosting will spread more easily.

2. Remove from freezer and assemble on a foil-covered board as illustrated (fig. 37b). Place cake piece B on top of piece A, using red frosting to attach. Slice C in half horizontally to create a piece (E) to place on the cab (D) to make it taller. Place C, D, and E as shown in fig. 37b. Frost between all layers with red frosting.

3. Frost on yellow windows as illustrated (fig. 37c). Frost the rest of the cake red.

4. Push the peppermint patties or

6. Place two white squares of gum on the front of the engine for headlights.

7. Use yellow gumdrops on top for the flashing lights.

Dalmatian Cupcakes

If time is short, bake a batch of cupcakes and frost them white. Put chocolate chips on top to resemble the spots on a dalmatian dog. If you want to make paw print cupcakes, stick a chocolate kiss in the center of a white cupcake and put three chocolate chips around the top of it.

Simple Fire Engine Cake

Frost a brown chocolate strip down the center of a sheetcake for a road. Use a frosting bag and a star tip to make grass out of green icing. For the lines down the center of the road use white or yellow candies. Place a toy fire engine on the road. If desired add other toy cars, toy street signs, houses, trees or people to the scale of the fire engine.

🎉 ARRIVAL 🎉 OF GUESTS

Before the party, make firefighter badges for nametags. The birthday child's could read, "Firechief Michael." The others could read, "Firefighter ___." Tape or pin these onto their shirts. Put a plastic firefighter hat on everyone as they arrive.

🎉 CRAFT 🎉

Dog Pictures

Trace the outline of a dog picture from a coloring book, and photocopy one picture for each guest. Supply the children with some paint or crayons and let them decorate their dogs anyway that they like. If they want their dog to have blue and red spots instead of dalmatian black, let them go for it.

🎉 GAMES AND 🎉 ACTIVITIES

Take a Trip to a Fire Station

Many fire stations give tours of their facilities. You could meet all of the children and their parents at your local fire department. Most fire stations have someone who will explain how things run, show you around and let the children get in the fire truck. Tours should be arranged in advance with the fire department, but be forewarned, a fire call can interrupt your tour. For the children, it is the highlight of the tour. Afterwards, bring everyone back home for some games, cake and ice cream.

If you have a friend or relative who is a firefighter, maybe that person could arrange to come to your home with a uniform on and talk a little bit about fire safety.

Firefighter Dressing Contest

You will need:

A pair of adult boots

Adult trousers with a pair of suspenders attached

An adult shirt

A plastic firefighter hat

A raincoat, optional

A stopwatch or a watch with a second hand

What to do:

Place all of the items on the floor and time the children to see who can get all of the clothes on the fastest. You may even choose to have two sets of these items and have two teams compete against one another. Write down all of the scores. The fastest child or team wins.

Put Out the Fire!

You will need:

A large heavy-duty cardboard box

Black, orange, red and yellow paint

A craft knife

A garden hose with a nozzle for aiming or a powerful water gun

A stopwatch or watch with a second hand

What to do:

1. Before the party, cut out the bottom of the box. Using the craft knife, cut out windows on one side of the box. Cut only three sides of the window so that it is more like a flap.

2. Paint the box black and paint flames on the windows.

3. During the party, close the flaps on the box, but not tightly, and mark on the ground where the children will need to shoot from. Test the water pressure and distance until you get it right. The water pressure shouldn't be so strong that it knocks over the entire box, just enough to open the "windows."

4. Line the children up behind the line and have them take turns trying to shoot open the windows or put out the "flames." Each child gets 10 seconds. The one to get the most open wins.

Rescue

You will need:

Toy people, dogs and cats

2 buckets of two different colors or one marked #1 and the other marked #2

What to do:

1. Before the party, hide the toy people, dogs and cats around the house or party area.

2. During the party, divide the children into two equal teams and tell them that they are to "rescue" the people, dogs and cats. Show them which bucket is their team's bucket and set where all can get to it.

3. At the signal, all the children pretend that they are firefighters searching for people, dogs and cats in the house. As each child finds one, he is to run to his team's bucket and drop the toy in. For parties with older children, you may want to set a timer for 5 minutes. For parties with very young children, just let them search until you feel that all of the toys have been found. The team to "rescue" the most people and animals wins.

Hose Relay

You will need:

2 hoses

Rope or string

Toy fire engine siren, optional

What to do:

1. Coil each hose up and tie it with rope or string so that it will be easy to carry.

2. Divide the children into two teams and stand them behind a marked line.

3. At the signal (the sound of the fire engine siren), the first two children in line are to run with the hose to another marked spot 20–30 feet away, come back and give the hose to the next child in line.

4. The next child in line does the same. This continues until one team finishes first. They are declared the winning team.

Rescue Toss

You will need:

A large bath towel, beach towel or old sheet

Several old stuffed rag dolls or stuffed animals (choose ones without any sharp points)

What to do:

1. The children must choose one person to be their partner.

2. One adult must go to a porch above (not too high).

3. The adult asks the first two children to grab opposite ends of the towel or sheet and stand below the porch.

4. The adult at the porch drops down a stuffed doll or stuffed animal, and the two children must try to catch it with their towel or sheet. Each two team members to make a catch win a prize. If you have a large amount of stuffed animals you could allow each team two or more tries.

Note: If the ground outside is wet or dirty, you may have to cancel this game, or use a ball instead.

Stop-Drop-and-Roll Tag

Play this game as you would regular tag, but when a child is tagged he must stop, drop, and roll.

Water Brigade

See Pool and Beach Party game "Fill the Bucket Relay."

🎉 FAVOR AND 🎉 PRIZE IDEAS

Decorate red bags with pictures of dalmatians, or decorate plain paper bags with pictures of fire trucks or hydrants. Fill the bags with small fire trucks, small books about fire trucks, toy dalmatians, dalmatian cupcakes (see Food), red and white candies, red hot candies or fireball candy. Place a plastic firefighter hat on everyone.

Airplane Party

Has your child ever dreamed of soaring like an eagle? Does he love to make paper airplanes? Maybe he just had his first airplane ride and it thrilled him so much that he talks about becoming a jet pilot. Perhaps one of his relatives is or was a pilot and has told him some great stories. If any of these situations fit your child to the tee, then you may have landed in the right spot with this chapter. This is a party that will definitely lift everyone's spirits!

🎉 AIRPLANE 🎉 INVITATION

Make an invitation like the one illustrated (fig. 38) out of colorful construction paper. You could even make one on your computer with an airplane pulling a happy birthday banner, and the plane flying over a cloud that has "#9" written on it. Another good idea would be to write your invitation on plain white paper, fold the paper into a paper airplane and hand deliver it to your guest's home. Tell them to open it to read the message.

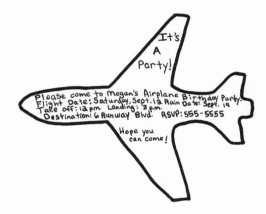

Fig. 38. Airplane Invitation

🎉 DECORATIONS 🎉

- Put a sign on the mailbox with an arrow that reads, "Airport this way →," and point it toward the house. Hang blue, gray and white balloons and crepe paper from the mailbox, front porch and in the party area.

- Make a sign out of cardboard or construction paper for the front door that reads, "Megan's International Airport" or "Party arrivals and departures at back gate."

- Hang foam or paper airplanes from light fixtures, keeping away from heat source. If your child has small plastic toy airplanes, they will work great too. Hang them with fishing line.

- Hang posters of airplanes on the walls such as the Blue Angels posters purchased at their air shows.

- Use a blue tablecloth and decorate it with silhouettes of airplanes cut from aluminum foil. Tape them on with masking tape. Use white plates, cups and napkins, or look for some with airplanes on them.

- If your child has a toy airplane, use it for a centerpiece.

- For placecards, put a sign on your child's chair that reads, "Captain Tony." On all of the other children's seats write "Co-pilot" and the guest's name.

- Play songs like "Leaving on a Jet Plane" (Peter, Paul and Mary), "High Flying Bird" (Elton John), "Magic Carpet Ride" (Steppenwolf — this song is great for the game Race to the Airport), "I Believe I Can Fly" (R. Kelly), "Wind Beneath My Wings" (Bette Midler), "Learning to Fly" (Tom Petty), "Riding in a Airplane" (Raffi) or "If I Could Only Fly" (Waylon Jennings).

🎉 FOOD 🎉

Serve the children their meals on their own "airplane trays" (pieces of cardboard) or real trays.

- Chicken wings
- Celery sticks, carrot sticks and ranch dressing for dipping
- Bread rolls or bread sticks
- Cheddar and mozzarella cheese chunks

Airport Runway Cake

You will need:

1 box cake mix, plus ingredients as box directs

3 cups green frosting

1 16 oz. can chocolate frosting

A marshmallow, or white pieces of Good & Plenty candy

Toy trees, optional

Small toy airplane

What to do:

1. Using a 9 × 13-inch pan, bake the cake and cool as directed. Freeze uncovered for at least an hour to make frosting spread more easily.

2. Frost a narrow runway strip (just wide enough for the plane) with the chocolate frosting.

3. Frost the rest of the cake green, using a decorator's bag and a star frosting tip to resemble grass.

4. Cut small slivers from the marshmallow for the lines on

the runway, or use the white candy pieces.

5. Place the airplane on the runway and place the toy trees on the grass.

Fluffy Clouds Cake

Frost a sheetcake blue and frost a white shell border along the top and bottom edge of the cake. Place a toy airplane on the cake and frost white streaks behind it. Frost white clouds above the airplane.

Airplane Cupcakes

If time is short, bake a batch of cupcakes and frost them blue. Place tiny toy airplanes on them.

ARRIVAL OF GUESTS

Use a kitchen timer to "beep" as guests go through airport security (your front door). As guests arrive, make them "check in" their baggage (coats, hats, purses, etc.) by taping a claim check to one of their items, or to the children, if it is too warm outside for coats and hats. On the back of each claim check write a number. At the end of the party have a drawing. The child whose number is called wins a prize.

CRAFTS

Making Paper Airplanes

You may be amazed at how many different ways the kids come up with to make their own unique paper airplanes. You may need to help those who have never made one before, but that shouldn't be too difficult. Many books can be found on the subject at libraries and bookstores. Making these airplanes should bring back memories from your own childhood paper airplane making days, or even a grandparents, if they are there helping you out. I was recently surprised to find out that my own father makes fascinating airplanes. The kid in you is sure to come out while making this craft — or should I say "aircraft."

You will need:

1 or more 8 × 12-inch pieces of plain white paper for each guest

One or two books on how to make paper airplanes

What to do:

1. As guests arrive, hand them a piece of paper and tell them to make a paper airplane. Show them the different types of models that they can make from the book, or see diagram (fig. 39a–e) for a basic paper airplane instruction. To make the basic paper airplane, first fold the sheet of paper in half lengthwise. Open it back up and fold in the two corners as shown with dotted line (fig. 39a).

2. Fold the two sides as shown along the dotted line, toward the center (fig. 39b).

3. Fold the paper completely in half so that the two sides meet (fig. 39c).

4. Fold one side down as shown along the dotted line (fig. 39d). Then do the other side. Unfold halfway (fig. 39e).

5. Write the children's names on their planes, and play the game Paper Airplane Landings, or simply let the children play with the planes. Let them experiment with a few different styles to see what types go faster than others do. Have fun!

♟ GAMES AND ♟ ACTIVITIES

Take a Trip to the Airport

Take a trip to the airport and watch the planes take off. It's free, except maybe for a parking fee at larger airports. Many small airports have picnic areas where you could eat or play games, or you could take everyone back to your house afterwards. For the brave at heart, consider chartering a plane to take the children up. Check to see if your local airports have a Young Eagles Program. At this time, it is run by the

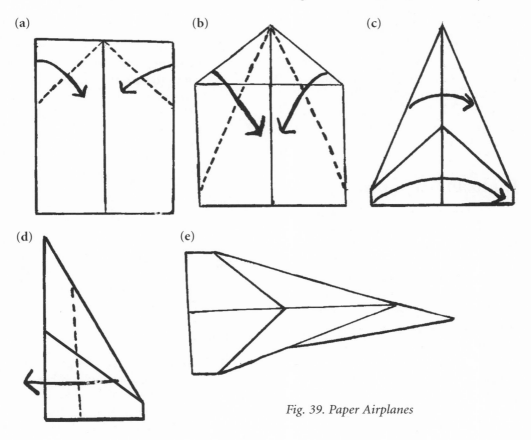

Fig. 39. Paper Airplanes

EAA Aviation Foundation, and it is a charitable non-profit organization. My son had a birthday party and took his friends on a flight at no cost through this program. It was a blast! The group of people who are volunteers through this program told me that they also do Boy Scout and Girl Scout troops all of the time. The reason this program was developed was to get young people interested in aviation. The pilots are required to be licensed and flights are conducted according to federal regulations. Only children between the ages of 8 and 17 may go. Permission slips from the parents are required to be filled out before going up. All parents enjoy staying and watching. They get nervous, but excited for their children. All enjoyed the event. The children all received a certificate after the flight. For more information on the Young Eagles Program you may either contact your local (smaller private) airports or contact the Young Eagles Office at: EAA Aviation Foundation, P.O. Box 2683, Oshkosh, WI 54903-2683 or call (414) 426-4831.

Go to an Air Show

If there will be an air show in town around the time of your child's birthday, you could take a few guests to see it. It would be a good idea to ask the parents to come and help you watch their children, or keep your group very small. It may be difficult to keep an eye on too many children. You wouldn't want to lose anyone.

Paper Airplane Landings

You will need:

Paper airplanes (see Crafts, "Making Paper Airplanes")
A tub
Prizes to go in the tub, optional

What to do:

1. After the children have made their paper airplanes, set up the tub. The best place to play this game is from a safe porch or deck, but it can be played at ground level. Place the tub approximately 15 feet away from a deck, porch or a marked throwing line. The wind conditions will determine the best distance for placing the tub.

2. Allow the children to all take turns throwing their paper airplanes toward the tub. Anyone who gets his plane into the tub gets to pick a prize out of the tub.

Soaring Paper Airplanes

You will need:

Two trees or two poles
A hula-hoop
2 pieces of rope
Paper airplanes (see Crafts, "Making Paper Airplanes")

What to do:

1. Tie one end of each rope to the hula-hoop, and tie the other ends to the trees or poles, suspending the hula-hoop between the two trees or poles.

2. Line the children up behind a marked throwing line, and have them take turns trying to get their paper airplanes to fly through the hoop. Anyone succeeding wins a prize.

Race to the Airport

You will need:

2 soft toy cars (preferably ones that look like yellow cabs) with no sharp points

Whistle

What to do:

1. Divide the children into two teams and stand them behind a marked start line. Set a goal 20–30 feet away.

2. Hand a car to the first child in each line. At the blow of a whistle, they must run to the goal and back, then pass the toy car to the next child in line.

3. The next child in line then does the same. This continues until one team has all of its members finish. They have made it to the airport and caught their plane!

Caution: Choose a soft toy car that does not have any sharp points, just in case someone should trip and fall on it while running.

Land the Airplane at the Airport

You will need:

An aerial picture of the ground below, complete with tree tops, houses, roads, etc. In the center

make an airport. Write "airport" on the roof.

Pictures of airplanes, made of construction paper or printed on a computer

Tape

A blindfold such as a scarf or a bandanna

What to do:

1. Before the party, write the children's names on the paper airplanes.

2. Hang the picture on a door or wall.

3. During the party, attach a loop of tape to the back of each plane.

4. Stand the children in a line. One at a time, blindfold each child, and turn them around three times.

5. Point the child in the general direction of the picture and have them "land" their airplane at the airport. Anyone landing on or close to the airport wins a prize.

Variation: You can also have the children try to land the planes on a runway strip.

Flight Attendant Relay

You will need:

2 serving trays or two pieces of cardboard, large enough to hold drink cans

1 empty drink can for each child, minus 2

Whistle

2 buckets

What to do:

1. Divide the children into two teams. Seat them in two single rows, on the ground or in chairs. Face everyone forward as if seated on a plane.

2. About 20–30 feet away from the first child in each line, place the buckets, and fill with one empty drink can for each team member, minus one can for each team.

3. Hand the first two children in line a tray or piece of cardboard. At the blow of the whistle, they must run to the bucket, put all of the cans onto their tray, go back to their team and pass out one can to each team member. They must do this without dropping the cans. If they drop them, they must stop, pick up the cans and put them back onto their tray.

4. After completing this, they then pass the tray off to the next child in line and go to the back of the line to sit down. The rest of the children all move forward one seat.

5. Then the next child in line must collect all of the empty cans, put them on their tray, take them to the bucket, put them in the bucket and then take the tray back to the next child in line. This continues on in this manner, one child passing the cans out and the next collecting them, until the first team to have all of its team members finish wins.

Balloon Jet Race

You will need:

Pieces of thread or string, each about 10–12 feet long, 1 per child

Balloons (plus a few extra, in case some pop), 1 per child

Drinking straws, 1 per child

Masking tape

Whistle

What to do:

1. Feed one thread or string through each straw, making sure that the straws can move easily along the strings. Make sure that all pieces of thread or string are exactly the same length. Attach one end of each string to something stationary such as chairs or a fence. Keep them all about 2–4 feet apart.

2. Attach a loop of tape to each end of each straw. (This is how you will attach the balloons to the straws in step 4.)

3. Line the children up in a row with each child in front of the free end of one thread or string.

4. Give each child one balloon. Have each child blow up his balloon so that it is equal in size to all of the other balloons. Instruct the children to hold the neck of the balloon closed tight and to be careful not to break the balloons. An adult must then attach the balloon to the tape on the straw, with the neck of the balloon facing the child.

5. At the blow of a whistle, all of

the children let go of their balloons. As the children release their balloons the blowing air will propel the balloons down the string. The child whose balloon reaches the end of the string first wins. An adult will need to watch closely for the winning balloon.

Note: Kids will probably want to play this more than once.

Bombs Away!

You will need:

A large piece of cardboard or wood
Several inflated balloons
Thumbtacks
Sharp darts

What to do:

1. Before the party, take all of the balloons and tack them to the cardboard or wood. Prop the board up against a garage wall or brick wall. Make sure that wherever you prop it is a safe place with nothing behind it — not your neighbor's yard with people or pets in it.

2. During the party, line the children up and allow them to take three shots at the balloons from about 5–6 feet back. Anyone to pop a balloon wins a prize.

Caution: Play this game only with children who are old enough to correctly aim the darts. Make sure that everyone is out of the way when the darts are thrown, including pets.

Plane Departure

You will need:

A soft toy airplane with no sharp points on it
A whistle or airplane-themed music

What to do:

1. Seat all of the children in a circle. Hand one child the airplane.

2. At the blow of the whistle or the start of the music, instruct the children to pass the airplane around in a clockwise direction.

3. When the whistle blows again or the music stops, the child stuck with the plane must "depart" — that is, he is out of the game. To prevent any hurt feelings, you might let him have a lollipop or control the music on the next round.

4. The game continues in this manner until the last two children are left. The one not stuck with the plane wins a prize.

Suitcase Packing Relay

You will need:

2 suitcases
Several items that you would pack on a trip (2 of everything): shirts, shorts, brush, comb, etc. You will need enough items so that each child in each of two lines can put one item in the suitcase.
Whistle, optional
Laundry basket

What to do:

1. Put equal amounts of each type of item in two laundry baskets. Put the suitcases about 20 feet away from the laundry baskets.

2. Line the children up in two equal lines behind the laundry baskets.

3. At the blow of the whistle, the first two children in each line must grab one item, race to their team's suitcase, put the item in the suitcase, run back to the next child in line and touch off.

4. The next child in line does the same. This continues until the first team finishes packing their suitcase. They are the winning team.

Gyrocopter Landings

You will need:

6½ × 1½-inch strips of paper, 1 per guest

Scissors

Paper clips, 1 per guest

What to do:

1. Starting at one end, cut a 3-inch slit down through the middle of the strip to create a pair of wings. (Do not cut the other end.)

2. Fold down the wings in opposite directions from one another. Now it should look like the blades of a helicopter.

3. Attach a paper clip to the bottom of the strip, for weight.

4. Mark an "X" on the ground. Allow the children to drop their gyrocopters from an elevated spot. The gyrocopters will spin down to the ground. Anyone landing on the "X" wins a prize (or give a prize to the one who comes closest).

🎉 FAVOR AND 🎉 PRIZE IDEAS

Small toy planes, plastic parachute people, foam airplane kits, airplane stickers, airplane erasers, airplane shaped cookies, airplane posters, small bags of peanuts (put a note on each bag that reads, "Thank you for flying ____ Airlines"), wing pins or pencils with airline logos on them (call your local airport to see if they have any) or Airheads candy.

Magic Party

Was your child's birthday here before you could say abracadabra? Well, here in this chapter is a party that doesn't require a lot of planning. It is simple, yet still fun. Most children love magic, but even more so when they are a part of the show. At this party, all will have an opportunity to be a magician and show their stuff. If you practice the tricks in this chapter, you are sure to mystify and amaze your guests. Before the party, rent some movies on magicians such as Houdini, or rent tapes that show you how to do some great tricks, and get in the spirit of becoming a magician. Read on for some magical ingredients to a spellbinding party!

🎉 MAGICIAN HAT 🎉 INVITATION

Cut this invitation out of black construction paper in the shape of a magician's hat as illustrated on next page (fig. 40a). Cut another shape the same size out of white paper. Write your birthday message on the white paper as illustrated (fig. 40b) and glue it to the black paper hat. On the other side of the hat, write a message as illustrated (fig. 40a) with a bottle of yellow glitter fabric and craft paint (the kind with a small pointed tip for writing). When the paint dries, this really looks great with the black background. Or if you like, you can write your message in glue and pour glitter over the glue. Shake off the excess glitter and allow to dry. You can even add star stickers to your invitation, for an extra touch.

Another invitation idea would be to make a yellow star shaped invitation. Use a star shaped cookie cutter, a stencil or even a children's toy sheriff badge to trace the star shape. Write the message shown in figure 40. Jazz the invitation up with some glitter to really get your guests' attention!

For parties with older children, ask each guest to come prepared to show a magic trick of their own.

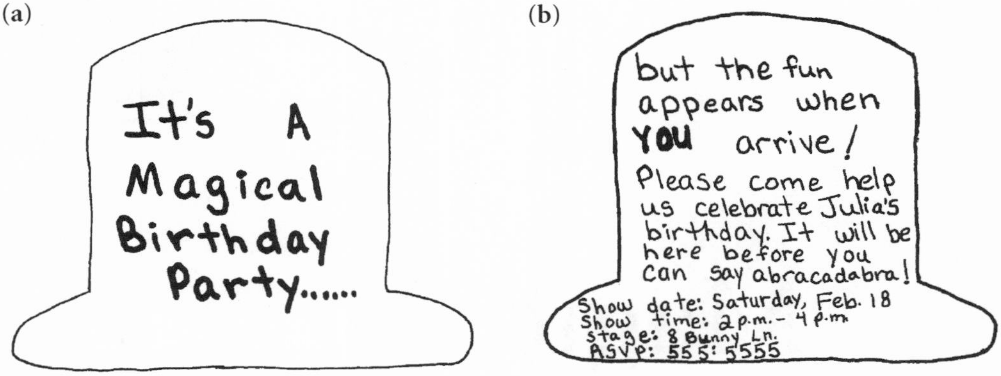

(a)

It's A Magical Birthday Party......

(b)

but the fun appears when **you** arrive!
Please come help us celebrate Julia's birthday. It will be here before you can say abracadabra!
Show date: Saturday, Feb. 18
Show time: 2 p.m.– 4 p.m.
Stage: 8 Bunny Ln.
RSVP: 555-5555

Fig. 40. Magician Hat Invitation

☆ DECORATIONS ☆

- Decorate the mailbox, front porch and party area with yellow, red and black balloons and crepe paper streamers.

- Put a star on the front door made of yellow construction paper that reads, "ABRACADABRA!"

- Make star and crescent (¼) moon shapes out of cardboard and cover them with aluminum foil. Punch a hole through the top of each one and suspend from the porch entrance, doorways, light fixtures (away from heat) and ceilings with fishing line.

- Make magician hat shapes out of black construction paper. Make rabbit figures out of white and pink construction paper, or print them on a computer. Hang these on walls and doors.

- Decorate the table with black, yellow and red tablecloth, plates, cups and napkins.

- For a centerpiece, place a black magician's top hat in the center of the table. Inexpensive plastic magician's hats can be purchased at party supply stores, magic stores, hobby shops and some toy stores. Place a stuffed bunny rabbit into the hat as if it is peeking out from the inside of the hat. Another centerpiece idea would be to spread out a deck of cards in a fan shape.

- Set up a magician's table. Use a card table, and cover it with a tablecloth (if you have a red tablecloth that would be great). If desired, tape yellow star and crescent moon shapes to the tablecloth. Place tricks and props underneath the table.

- If you just happen to have an old tux or fancy dress hanging around your house, wear it while performing your magic tricks. Why not get some use out of it? Play the part of a real magician!

- Play songs like "Abracadabra" (Steve Miller), "Magic" (Pilot), "Magic Carpet Ride" (Steppenwolf), "Black Magic Woman" (Santana) or "It's Magic" (Craig 'n Co.).

♟ FOOD ♟

Serve foods with a surprise inside of them or a food that the children must guess the contents of before you cut it open, or before they bite into it.

- Chicken pot pie (a whole pie or individual frozen pies)
- Green salad

— or —

- Fajitas (have the meat done and in a pot, ready to go; set out toppings and let guests help themselves)
- Tortilla chips
- Salsa (mild)

Star Cake

This cake is so yummy looking that it will disappear before you can say abracadabra! If desired, stick a few star stickers on the serving board. Use trick candles that relight for this cake (not the sparkler-type, if using the star stickers). Have a cup of water handy for extinguishing them.

A star shaped cake pan can be purchased at many kitchen supply stores or craft stores, but if you can't find one, follow the directions below to make a star shaped cake without a star shaped pan.

You will need:

1 box of cake mix, plus ingredients as box directs
3–4 cups of bright yellow frosting
Aluminum foil, optional
Blue plastic wrap, optional
Star stickers, optional

What to do:

1. Using two 8- or 9-inch round pans, bake two cake layers as directed. Cut one layer into five equal triangles as diagram on next page shows (fig. 41a) and leave the other layer whole. Trim the curved side of each section slightly inward. Trim just enough so that each section will fit snugly against the remaining round layer. Use a round cake pan edge as a guide for cutting.

2. Freeze uncovered for about one hour to make the frosting spread more easily.

3. Remove the cake from the freezer and assemble it on a board that has been covered with aluminum foil and then blue plastic wrap. This will give the appearance of a sky.

4. Assemble the cake at one end of the board, leaving room for the shooting streaks. First frost the inner sides and attach them to the round cake, forming a star as shown in diagram (fig. 41b). Then frost the entire cake yellow. Frost yellow shooting streaks behind the cake to make it look like a shooting star.

5. Place star stickers on the blue plastic wrap.

(a)   (a)   (b)

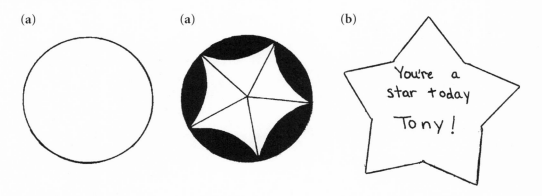

Fig. 41. Shooting Star Cake

🎩 ARRIVAL 🎩 OF GUESTS

As guests arrive at the door, hold a black magician's top hat in your hand. Have a piece of candy hidden in the hat for each guest. (Use a silk scarf to conceal the candy.) Tell the children to tap your hat twice and say the magic word — but they have to guess what the magic word is! (It's "abracadabra.") If they cannot guess, point to your "ABRACADABRA!" sign hanging on the front door, if using one, and if the child can read. Once they guess the magic word (and even if they don't), give them a piece of candy. That should start the guest off in the right mood for what is to come!

🎩 CRAFTS 🎩

Magic Wands

You will need:

1 can of spray paint, either silver, black or blue

½-inch diameter wooden dowels, 1 foot long, 1 per guest

Red and yellow plastic tape

Star stickers, optional

What to do:

1. Before the party, spray paint the dowels with the color of choice. Allow to dry.

2. During the party, let guests wrap the yellow tape around the sticks to look like a spiral, or they may put stickers on their wands.

3. Wrap the ends of the wands with two strips of red tape, and Presto! You now have a magic wand!

Variation: If desired, make yellow construction paper or posterboard stars, and decorate with glitter glue. Tape or hot glue the stars to the top of the wands. Just don't let the children get near the hot glue.

Write with Invisible Ink

See Mystery Party.

⚜ GAMES AND ⚜ ACTIVITIES

If you don't want to put on a magic show yourself, consider asking a friend, relative or perhaps a teenage neighbor who is good at performing magic tricks to do it. You may be surprised to find out how many of your friends know great magic tricks. Another option is to hire a magician. Check your local phone book, newspapers or Internet sites (under party planning).

Some tips before doing any tricks:

1. Practice your tricks before the day of the party. Make sure that you have them down, so that you keep your guests' interest.

2. Before doing any tricks, ask any of the guests if they have ever seen the trick that you are about to perform. If they have, remind them to keep the trick a secret because it won't be any fun if they spills the beans. Ask them to whisper what they think the trick is in your ear. If they are correct, let them have a turn at amazing the audience with the trick.

3. Don't show or tell your tricks to the birthday child as you're learning them. That way, the day of party he will be just as surprised as everyone else, maybe even a bit proud of you and your fascinating tricks!

Magic Balls

I love this trick. It is so simple, yet it never fails to impress your audience!

You will need:

3 plastic disposable drinking cups, all the same size, and of a dark, nontransparent color

1 ball only *slightly* smaller than the rim of your cups

1 table

What to do:

1. Place all of your cups upside down on the table.

2. Show your audience the ball, and place the ball underneath one of the cups.

3. Switch the cups around and around, quickly. Tell the audience to keep their eyes on the cup with the ball. Hold the cups firmly, so that you can feel the ball underneath the cup. This is how you will know where it is.

4. Stop switching the cups. Ask an audience member to *point to* a cup that they guess the ball is in. Remind them that they are *not* to lift the cup! (Otherwise they will spoil the trick.)

5. If the guest has pointed to the cup that contains the ball, squeeze its sides as you pick up the cup so that you lift the ball up with the cup. The cup will appear empty! Never lift the cup so that they can see the ball. Always lift it straight up. If the cup that they choose is empty, also slightly squeeze

that cup, otherwise they will catch on that the cup that is squeezed is the one with the ball.

6. Place the cup back onto the table, and repeat the trick as many times as you like.

Mind Reader

This trick is for children 6 and over. Any younger and they won't get it. To perform this trick you will need an assistant to help you. Discuss the trick with the assistant before the party. (See step 4.)

You will need:

A deck of cards

A magic wand or a stick

What to do:

1. Tell the guests that you can read their minds. Spread 9–12 cards out onto the floor or a table.

2. Turn your back, and ask one of the audience members to touch one of the cards while your back is turned. At this time, your assistant must watch and see which card is touched.

3. Then turn around and tell everyone to concentrate on the chosen card, but not to look at it.

4. Before the party, you will have instructed the assistant to touch all of the wrong cards on the left side with a magic wand and to touch all of the correct ones on the right side. Be sure that you are both standing on the same side of the table. Your assistant first points the magic wand at a few wrong cards on the left side and asks, "Is this the one?" You then answer, "No." When the pointer finally touches one on the right side you answer "Yes." Your audience will be amazed!

Blacks and Reds

This is a very easy trick that your child might enjoy doing.

You will need:

A deck of cards

What to do:

1. Arrange a deck of cards by putting all of the black cards on one half of the deck and all of the reds on the other half.

2. Ask an audience member to pick a card and look at it, but not to show it to you. They may show it to the audience. As the card is pulled from the deck, watch to see if the card comes from the top or bottom of the deck.

3. Take the card back without looking at it, and slide it into the other half of the deck.

4. Fan the cards out a bit, facing you, and announce that you will now find the card. Then do so! (All you have to do is look for one that doesn't match the color of the cards around it.)

Magic Ribbon

At first the instructions to this trick may seem complicated, but after you have done it once you realize how very simple and yet amazing this trick is. It really got me the first time it was shown to me. I could not figure it out for the life of me!

You will need:

An ordinary envelope
A pair of scissors
A piece of ribbon, 14 inches long

What to do:

1. Before the party, cut a ¼-inch strip off each end of the envelope. Then cut a slot slightly bigger than the ribbon in the back, middle, of the envelope. Seal the envelope closed.

2. Slip the ribbon through the envelope, leaving about 2¼ inches of ribbon sticking out from both ends.

3. Pull a little loop of the ribbon out from the slot in the back of the envelope.

4. During the party, hold the envelope in one hand (uncut side facing the audience — do not show the slot on the back) and the scissors in the other. Show the envelope to your audience, and tell them that you will cut the envelope in half without cutting the ribbon. *Or* tell your audience that you will cut the ribbon in half and then magically put the ribbon back together after it has been cut.

5. Bend the envelope in half with

the hand that is holding it, so that the slotted side of the envelope remains facing in towards your body, unseen by your audience. The uncut side must always face toward the audience.

6. Take the scissors and slowly cut the envelope, being very careful to cut *under* the loop of ribbon. Make sure that you do not cut the ribbon.

7. When the cutting is done, the envelope will be in two pieces. Straighten up the envelope, keeping it held together at the center with one hand, so that the audience cannot see the ribbon in the center.

8. If you are going to use an assistant, now is the time to have your assistant say some magic words, and fool your audience into thinking that you have magically put the ribbon back together.

9. Grab the end of the ribbon that is visible to the audience, and pull it out quickly. Your guests will be surprised that the ribbon has been magically mended!

Card Toss

You will need:

1 or 2 decks of playing cards
Magician's top hat or a bucket
String or chalk

What to do:

1. Place the hat or bucket on the floor or ground. Place the string

in a large circle around the hat about 5 feet away (or draw a circle with the chalk if playing on the pavement).

2. Divide the children into two equal teams. Have them stand in a circle around the hat, each team making up half the circle. Hand one team all of the black cards (dividing them equally among the children) and hand the other team all of the red cards.

3. Begin with the birthday child, and ask him to toss all of his cards (one at a time) into the hat or bucket. It is best to sort of fling them downward (not towards anyone's face), sort of Frisbee style.

4. Then proceed clockwise until all of the guests have had a turn to toss all of their cards. The team with the most colors in the hat or bucket wins.

Variation: Line the children up single file, and allow each child 4 shots of the cards. The child to get the most cards into the hat or bucket wins a prize.

Vanishing Coin Trick

Now here's a trick that will blow away your audience!

You will need:

A silver dollar (use a half dollar if you can't get a silver dollar)

A clear glass full of water (but not full to the top); the inside diameter should be the size as the coin

A clear, round, flashlight lens about the same size as the coin

A dark colored handkerchief or bandanna (not transparent)

What to do:

1. Place the glass of water on a table or countertop. Stick the clear flashlight lens under the handkerchief when there is no one around to see you do it. Fold the handkerchief in half, holding the lens in it, and set it on the table or countertop next to the glass. Do this either before the party, or after everyone has left the room for another activity.

2. Bring everyone into the room and show everyone the coin, the glass of water and the handkerchief, and tell them that you are going to make the coin vanish.

3. Tell the audience that you are going to place the coin under the handkerchief and make it disappear. Use both hands to place the coin into the handkerchief, and pull the coin out with one hand while it is concealed in the palm of your hand. Keep your hand with the coin to your side, so that it isn't seen. The clear flashlight lens still in its place will look like the coin.

4. Keeping the lens covered with the handkerchief, but letting the audience see its shape, pick up lens and handkerchief together with your thumb and forefinger. Drape the handkerchief over the glass, holding the lens over the water, still gripping it with your fingers.

5. Then say to the audience, "Now you see the coin is still under the handkerchief, and to prove it to you I will choose an audience member to come up and feel the coin." At this time choose someone to come up and feel the coin, to verify that you indeed have a "coin" under the handkerchief. The flashlight lens will look and feel like the coin.

6. Then tell them that you are going to drop the coin into the water and make it vanish. Drop the flashlight lens into the water while the glass is still covered with the handkerchief. The audience will hear it drop in and think that the coin is in the water. Ask the audience, "Where is the coin now?" and all will answer, "In the glass!" Now tell them that you are going to make it disappear.

7. Wave a magic wand over the still-covered glass, and say a few magic words. This will give the lens a moment to work its way down to the bottom of the glass and settle into place.

8. Lift away the handkerchief and the coin will appear to have vanished. Actually, at this time it is at the bottom of the glass, and very difficult to see. *Slowly* pour the water from the glass to prove that the coin is not in the glass. The flashlight lens will stick to the bottom of the glass and no one will be the wiser!

🎉 FAVOR AND 🎉 PRIZE IDEAS

Small stuffed bunny rabbits, inexpensive plastic magicians' top hats, magic playing cards or ordinary playing card sets, colorful scarves (complete with disappearing directions), rabbit shaped candy, magicians' wands (see Crafts), magic trick books, inexpensive magic trick sets, star shaped cookies, magnets or magical paint-with-water books.

Mystery Party

I spy a great time! And so will your child and his friends when they transform themselves into secret agents. At this party, the children will take on roles of bomb squad agents, detectives, victims, suspects, witnesses and mystery solvers. This is a party that helps sharpen listening, memory and problem solving skills...but the children will be having so much fun that they will never even realize that they are learning! Before the party, rent movies like *Harriet the Spy*, *The Great Mouse Detective*, Alfred Hitchcock movies or Sherlock Holmes movies to help get your family in the spirit. Read on to solve the mystery of giving a great party!

♟ MYSTERY ♟ INVITATION

There are too many great invitation ideas for this type of party for me to give you just one! Here are several invitation ideas sure to grab any guest's attention. On the outside of the mailing envelope for any of these invitations write the words "TOP SECRET."

- Cut out letters from newspapers or magazines and piece together the words on your invitation, like a ransom note. Glue them on paper.

- Fold a piece of paper in half, like a card, and put question marks all over the front of the invitation. Write your message on the inside of the invitation.

- Paint old puzzles white (use small ones that are not too difficult). With felt tip marker or paint write out your invitation. Blank white puzzles can be found at some party supply stores. If you don't have any old puzzles, or don't want to paint the ones that you have, write your invitation on posterboard. Cut the posterboard to look like a puzzle. Put the invitation in an envelope and hand-deliver it. You may want to tell your guests that it is a birthday party invitation, so that it does not get set aside. Tell them that they must piece together the invitation to read the message.

- Write your invitation letters backwards and instruct your guests to hold the invitation up to a mirror to read it.

- Cut up a large sheet of Fun Foam (found in craft stores) into a puzzle. Write guests' names on puzzle pieces.Write your invitation on a piece of paper instructing the guests to bring the puzzle piece included to the party. Explain that they are the missing piece to your puzzle, and that your party won't be complete unless they can come to fit the puzzle piece with the rest of the pieces.

- Write your invitation message in a secret code and include a piece of paper with a decoding key. (Make sure that you also include an actual invitation, for those who can't decode your message!)

- Hang pictures of Sherlock Holmes hats, pipes and magnifying glasses (make them from a computer).

- Decorate pieces of paper to look like the covers of popular mystery books and hang in the party area.

- Use a white tablecloth and tape black and red question marks all over it. Use black and red tableware.

- For placemats, use mazes from coloring books by ripping a page out for each guest.

- Use mystery novels and a magnifying glass for a centerpiece.

- Play theme songs from current detective shows, or play songs like "Alfred Hitchcock Presents" (Arthur Fiedler/The Boston Pops), "Twilight Zone" (Neil Norman) or "Dragonet" (Stan Fredburg). The last title is a really funny spoof on the *Dr. Demento's 20th Anniversary Collection*. The children would love it.

▲ DECORATIONS ▲

- Decorate your mailbox, front porch and party area with black, red and white balloons and crepe paper streamers.

- Trace the soles of your shoes onto black or brown construction paper. Cut out the shapes and place them along your sidewalk leading to your front door.

- Make a large question mark out of black construction paper and hang it on your front door.

- Hang paper question marks made of various colors all over your house.

▲ FOOD ▲

Foods with hidden fillings would fit this theme very well. Let the children try to guess what is inside before eating it. Some possibilities:

- Filled raviolis
- Bread sticks

— or —

- Fajitas (have the meat done and in a pot, ready to go; set out toppings and let guests help themselves)
- Tortilla chips
- Salsa (mild)

Mystery Cake

Bake and cool a sheetcake as directed. For parties with older children, cut a small slit anywhere in the cake and hide a jellybean or a peanut in the slit. Frost the cake white. Use colorful icing, a decorator's bag, and a small round frosting tip to pipe question marks all over the cake. If desired, use trick candles that relight for this cake. Have a cup of water handy for extinguishing them. After singing "Happy Birthday" and before passing out the cake, tell everyone to be careful because there is a hidden jellybean or peanut inside one of the pieces of cake. The child who finds it wins a prize! An appropriate prize would be a small bag of peanuts or jellybeans.

Note: You may want to hide two peanuts or jellybeans in the cake. Hide one on each end of the cake, just in case no one gets a slice with the peanut. Just be prepared to give two prizes, in case two should win.

CRAFTS

Write with Invisible Ink

You will need:

A bowl
A bottle of lemon juice
Iodine
Medium jar half full of water and labeled "poisonous"
Paint brushes, 1 per child
Sheets of white paper, at least 1 per child

What to do:

1. Pour some lemon juice into the bowl.
2. Add a little iodine to the jar of water and mix it.
3. Hand each child a paintbrush and a sheet of paper. Tell them to dip the paintbrush in the lemon juice and write a "secret message" on their paper with the lemon juice. Allow the lemon juice to dry.
4. After the secret messages have dried, have the children brush the paper with the iodine mixture. The iodine makes the invisible writing appear on the paper!

Caution: DO NOT leave children unattended around the iodine mixture. It is poisonous if ingested.

Dusting for Fingerprints

This is a messy craft, so you may choose to do it outdoors and near the end of the party. It is also best to do it after everyone one has eaten. Sticky fingers make better fingerprints!

You will need:

Sandpaper
Pencil
Disposable bowl
Clear glass jars, 1 per guest
A small dry paintbrush
A small amount of cooking oil (if the children's hands aren't sticky enough)

What to do:

1. Before the party, rub the pencil lead across the sandpaper many

times, to create a powder, and pour the powder into the disposable bowl. Cover until needed.

2. During the party, have the children touch the glass jar to get their fingerprints on it.

3. Put some pencil lead powder on the paintbrush and *tap* (don't brush on) a tiny amount of powder over the fingerprints on the glass. The children's fingerprints will appear! If the children's fingers are too clean (fat chance!) for the fingerprints to show up, then rub a small amount of oil onto their fingers and try it again.

4. As soon as you have finished, dispose of the powder and wash everyone's hands thoroughly. Rinse the glass jars with soapy water or dispose of them.

Note: This may also be done with talcum powder, but it doesn't show up as well as the pencil lead.

🎉 GAMES AND 🎉 ACTIVITIES

Who Done It?

Read the children short story mystery books. See who can figure out the answers to the mysteries. One good book to get is a book called *Almost Perfect Crimes* by Hy Conrad.

Solve the Mystery

Tell the children the following story and see if they can figure out the correct answer to solve the mystery. You will get many good answers, but the child who gets the correct answer wins. You may give clues, if necessary.

Story: A man and a woman went on a vacation. Two months after they returned from their vacation, they told the police that they had found the missing dead body that the police had been searching for in the area where they had been vacationing. Then the police asked the couple why it took them two months to report that they knew where the body was.

Question: Why *did it* take the couple two months to report that they had found the missing body?

Answer: The man took a picture of his wife, and it took them two months to develop the film. When they were looking at their picture they noticed the dead body in the background.

Scavenger Hunt

When I was a teenager we had scavenger hunts that were much more difficult than the following. The scavenger hunts usually involved getting in our cars and searching for odd items as teams. If you will be having a mystery party for teenagers, you can change the rules a little. Make the hunt more detailed and complicated to make it more fun for older children. For parties with younger children, remind the children that they are to stay in your yard, and tell them that all of the items can be found in your home or yard.

You will need:

> A list of items to be found around
> your house, 1 per team (e.g., a
> pinecone, 3 rocks, something red,
> etc.)
>
> Pencils, 1 per team
>
> Large paper grocery bags, 1 per team

What to do:

Divide the children into two equal teams and hand each group a list of items, a pencil, and a bag to hold the items that they are to search for. Tell the children that they are to search around the house, either indoors or outdoors, for all of the items on their list. Once they find the items, they are to cross them off the list. Send them searching! Set a time limit of about 15 minutes to find what is on the list. The team to find the most items on the list when the time is up wins.

Photographic Memory

This is a game that can be played while everyone is seated to eat.

You will need:

> Various items: spoon, ball, scissors,
> pen cap, pencil, paper clip, dice,
> crayon, barrette, playing card, etc.
>
> A serving tray or cookie sheet
>
> Sheets of paper, 1 per guest
>
> Pencils, 1 per guest

What to do:

1. Seat all of the children in a circle around a table or on a floor, and give each child a piece of paper and a pencil.

2. Place all of the items on the tray or cookie sheet and set it in the center of the table or circle of children. Ask the children to study the items carefully.

3. Ask them to close their eyes as you remove one item and hide it behind your back.

4. Tell them to open their eyes and *write down* (not shout out!) what they guess is missing.

5. Repeat the sequence several times. The child with the most correct guesses wins.

Who's Missing?

1. Choose one child to be "It," and have him sit in a chair with his back facing the rest of the children.

2. To begin the game, It must cover his eyes. One of the guests then quietly leaves the room and hides out of It's sight.

3. Once the child is hidden, tell It to turn around and try to see who is missing from the group. If It guesses correctly, the player who left the room is It for the next round. If the guess is wrong, It turns around again, covers his eyes and the missing child returns to the room.

4. It turns back around again and gets 3 more guesses as to which child has returned. If the guesses are all incorrect, the other players provide 3 clues and then the answer. Continue by choosing another child to be

It, and play in this manner for as long as time allows.

Mystery Present

You will need:

Several boxes of various sizes

Plenty of wrapping paper or colored tissue paper

Tape

Music

What to do:

1. Before the party, place a small prize in a small box and wrap it with wrapping paper or tissue paper. Place that box inside of another box and also wrap it with wrapping paper or tissue paper. Repeat this several times with various size boxes until you have one large wrapped "present" with many other boxes inside.

2. During the party, seat all of the players in a circle and hand the "present" to the birthday child, but tell him that he is not to open it.

3. Begin playing the music, and have the children pass the present around the circle in a clockwise direction. When the music stops, the child holding the present must unwrap the present — but only as far as the next box.

4. Begin the music again, and have them continue as before. The player who gets down to the last box with the prize in it, and unwraps it, gets to keep it.

Note: You may use newspaper to wrap the boxes, if you want to save on the expense of wrapping paper, but the newspaper is messy on the hands. It may be a good problem to have, though, if you are doing the craft "Dusting for Fingerprints" afterwards!

Puzzle Contest

You will need:

A simple puzzle (not too easy and not too hard)

A stopwatch or secondhand

Paper

Pencil

What to do:

Jumble up all of the puzzle pieces and lay them face up on the table. The children all take turns trying to put the puzzle together. Set the stopwatch, and tell them to go at a signal. Write each child's time down. The child to finish in the quickest amount of time wins.

Scotland Yard

This is a game played by children in England, where it is also called "Detective" or "Murder." This game must be played at night, and preferably in a large open area without any obstacles.

You will need:

Slips of paper, 1 per guest

A hat

Pen or pencil

What to do:

1. Before the party, write "detective" on one slip of paper. Write "the killer" on another. Write

"witness" on all of the remaining slips of paper. Fold up all of the slips of paper and place them into the hat.

2. During the party, pass the hat around and have each player draw a slip of paper.

3. The child to draw "detective" identifies himself as the detective and leaves the room.

4. The child to draw "killer" tells the "witnesses" who he is. This is kept a secret from the detective.

5. The detective returns, takes a seat and the lights are turned off. All players but the detective are free to move around.

6. The killer tags someone in the dark, and the "victim" must scream. The victim plays dead.

7. A few seconds later the lights are turned on (an adult would be a good person to be in charge of the lights).

8. It is the detective's job to find out who the killer is. He can ask any player (except the victim, of course) a set amount of questions (decide before the game how many questions will be allowed). When questioned, the witnesses must tell the truth. They do not tell who the killer is, but they must answer questions such as the following examples:

   • Where were you standing in the room when the victim was murdered?

   • Did you hear any movements nearby, and if so

what did they sound like (e.g., squeaky tennis shoes, heels, noisy clothing, etc.)?

   • Was the noise to your right or your left?

   • Did you feel or hear someone walk by you, and if so in which direction did they go?

9. When the "detective" runs out of questions or thinks that he has his killer, he asks one last question of the player that he believes is the killer: "Did you kill the victim?" If the detective has guessed correctly, the killer must answer "yes." The detective only gets one shot at asking this question. If he guesses correctly, he is the winner, and gets a prize. If the detective guesses wrong, he is fired! Either way, the slips can go back in the hat and the game can be played again.

Caution: Before playing this game, clear the room of any sharp furniture or breakables, so that no one bumps into it or falls onto it while walking in the dark. Tell the children that when they play dead not to *fall* to the ground. Tell them to slowly get down onto the floor or chair, so that they don't hurt themselves.

I Spy

1. Choose one child to be "It." It says, "I spy with my little eye something red" (or square, blue, heavy, tall, long, etc.). He may use only one word to describe what he is looking at.

2. The children all must try to guess what it is that he has spied around the room or outside.

3. The player to guess correctly is the next It.

Ticking Time Bomb

You will need:

A kitchen timer

What to do:

1. Hide a kitchen timer inside of the house or outdoors. Set it to go off in about 3–5 minutes, depending on how well it is hidden and the age of the players finding it.

2. At the signal to go, the "bomb squad" (the children) search for the timer by listening carefully for the ticking sound. Remind the children that they must be very quiet to hear it. The one who finds it before it rings wins!

Variation: You may also divide the players into groups to search for the bomb. All of the team members work together to find it. The team to find it wins.

Police Lineup

You will need:

Large numbers written on pieces of paper

Tape or safety pins

1 pencil

Pieces of paper, 1 per guest

What to do:

1. Pin or tape a number to the front of each child's shirt. Have half of the children line up against a wall.

2. Have the other half carefully study all of the other players, then give them 5 minutes to turn around and write down as much about the other children as they can remember. Examples: #1 has brown eyes, brown hair, a red shirt and blue pants; #2 has red hair, blue eyes, a striped shirt and black pants; #3 has blond hair, blue eyes, a bandage on her knee and a purple dress with yellow polka dots. When the children are done, tell each to write his name at the top of his paper and to hand it to you.

3. Have the children switch places and continue as before. The child to get the longest correct list wins.

♟ FAVOR AND ♟ PRIZE IDEAS

Magnifying glasses, any type of "filled" candy, Cracker Jacks caramel popcorn (with a surprise inside of the box), puzzle books, puzzles, notepads, pens, pencils, detective comic books, detective disguises (false mustaches, plastic sunglasses and hats), or even the disguise glasses that come complete with a nose and mustache attached would be great.

Fashion Party

If fashion is your little girl's thing, then how about having a dress-up party? If your little girl just loves to dress up in fancy clothes and pretend that she is all grown up, then she'll just love this party! At this party the children come dressed in their fancy dress-up play clothing and pretend that they are beautiful models or famous actresses. It would be a good idea to talk to the parents of your child's friends before planning this party. Some of your child's friends may have a lot of dress-up play clothes and others may have none. This could cause a problem if the parent doesn't have anything to send their child in. If you have some extra dress-up clothes to loan to your guests, then let your guests know this. (Toy stores, jewelry and fashion accessory boutiques, thrift shops and mail order companies are a good source of fancy children's dress-up clothing and accessories.) Turn the pages to see how to put on an elegant dress-up party sure to make any young lady feel special!

FANCY SHOE INVITATION

Make a shoe shaped invitation like the one illustrated (fig. 42), using brightly colored paper. Cut a bow out of a shiny cloth material and glue it on, or brush on some glue in the shape of a bow and pour glitter over it. Cut an oval shape out of a different color such as yellow, for the inside of the shoe, and write, "Put on your fancy shoes and come to a dress-up party!" On the back of the shoe write your birthday message as illustrated. Be sure that the invitation lets the guests know that they are to dress up in their make-believe clothes.

DECORATIONS

- Decorate the mailbox, front porch and party area with pastel pink, pur-

166

(a)   (b)

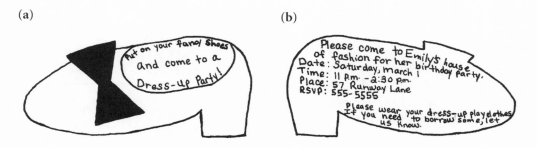

Fig. 42. Fancy Shoe Invitation

ple and silver or gray balloons and crepe paper streamers.

- Cut shoe and hat shapes out of construction paper or print them on a computer. Decorate them with glitter or ribbon and hang them on the walls or front door.

- Make a "walk of fame" sidewalk. Cut large yellow stars out of construction paper and write one guest's name on each star. Stick the stars to your sidewalk by putting a few loops of masking tape on the backside of each one. Face them so that the guests can read them as they walk up your sidewalk.

- Put a fancy tablecloth on the table and use nice napkins, dishes, teacups and silverware, or use pretty disposable tableware.

- For a centerpiece, put a vase of fresh flowers on the table and give each guest a flower to take home as a party favor at the end of the party.

- Play upbeat music as guests arrive, or play songs like the theme song from the Miss America Pageant. Some great songs to play are "Snapshot" (Ru Paul), "The Catwalk" (various artists), "Blue Suede Shoes" (Elvis Presley), "Hair" (The Cowsills), "You Wear It Well" (Rod Stewart), "Diamonds Are a Girl's Best Friend" (Marilyn Monroe — look under the movie/show tunes or Broadway musical category), "Buttons and Bows" (Gene Autry), "Isn't She Lovely" (Stevie Wonder) or "Hi-Diddle-Dee-Dee, an Actor's Life for Me" (from the Disney *Pinocchio* soundtrack).

♣ FOOD ♣

- Croissant sandwiches: fill with ham, cheese (Swiss or provolone), mayonnaise or mustard

- Bow tie pasta salad

- Vegetable sticks: serve with ranch dressing for dipping

- Chocolate covered strawberries or a couple of tea cookies such as Russian teacakes

- Tea or apple juice, served from an elegant teapot into fancy teacups (if serving tea, provide lemon wedges, honey and sugar)

- Candy and nuts (in small fancy bowls on the coffee table for guests to munch on during the party).

Doll Cake

You will need:

A 2-quart, half oval shaped, oven-proof batter bowl

1 box of cake mix (8–9 ounces), plus ingredients as box directs

3–4 cups of icing

Food coloring

Doll pick (found at craft or kitchen supply store)

Cake decorating flowers (found in the baking aisle of grocery stores), optional

What to do:

1. Prepare cake batter according to package directions and pour into the greased and floured ovenproof batter bowl. Bake 55–65 minutes or until a cake tester or wooden skewer inserted in the center comes out clean.

2. Cool 15 minutes on a cooling rack and invert onto a serving platter or a foil-covered board. Cool 3–4 hours before decorating.

3. Insert the bottom half of a doll pick into the top of the cake.

4. Frost the cake to look like a gown or a dress. Decorate the skirt part (the cake) with flowers and ribbons. Use a rose tip to make flowing ribbons across the skirt. Make flowers to put on top of the ribbons using a frosting tip or buy store-bought cake decorating flowers. Finish off the dress by frosting a bodice on the doll body using a small star tip.

⚜ ARRIVAL ⚜ OF GUESTS

As the guests arrive, give anyone who needs to borrow some dress-up clothes an outfit to put on. Show them to a bedroom or bathroom that they may get dressed in. Ask their parents to help them, if necessary. Ask their parents if it is o.k. to put any make-up or perfume on their child. Pretty everyone up by painting their nails, putting on a little lipstick, doing their hair up, etc. Put facial make-up on with a new cotton swab for each child, for sanitary reasons. You may want to ask a friend to help you with this. Ask a friend who is a hairstylist, or someone who is really good at doing hair and make-up, to come and help you. Having two or three people fixing everyone up at a time can help speed things up. If you need to use any hair accessories, give them to children as party favors. As the girls are being made up, have another person "interview" them and write down information about them for the activity "Fashion Show."

Take a Trip to a Beauty Salon

Some beauty salons have birthday party packages that let you bring in your guests for a makeover. The children can have their hair curled or done fancy. Some places will do makeup and nail polish. Afterwards, some will give the children a balloon and a surprise. You wouldn't want to eat your cake and ice cream at a beauty salon (unless, of course, they have a separate place for you to go), so take the guests out to a restaurant afterwards or back to your home for a party.

🎉 CRAFTS 🎉

Pasta Jewelry

You will need:

Tube shaped pasta such as rigatoni or ziti

Spray paint in one or more colors: glossy gold, silver, red, blue, yellow, etc.

Newspaper

Elastic string (found at a craft or fabric store)

Plastic disposable bowls

Scissors

What to do:

1. Before the party, lay the pasta out on the newspaper (outdoors) and spray paint it in the color that you choose. Allow the noodles to dry, and then turn them over, spray paint the other side, and again allow to dry. Place the pasta in disposable bowls until the party.

2. During the party, set the bowls of painted pasta, elastic string and scissors out onto the table. Let the children string the pasta onto cut pieces of the elastic string. Make long necklaces or small bracelets. Tie the ends of the elastic string together and clip off the excess.

Variation: Purchase jewelry beads

at a craft store and let the children use them in place of the pasta.

Fancy Hats

You will need:

Inexpensive straw hats

Hat decorations: ribbon, feathers, artificial flowers, sequins, beads, etc.

Glue

Scissors

Newspaper or a paper tablecloth

What to do:

Lay the newspaper or paper tablecloth out onto a table to protect the table. Lay out all of the supplies and let the guests decorate their own fancy party hats. You might want to have a pretty sample hat set out on the table to show them how they can make one look.

Paper Plate Hats

See Teddy Bear Tea Party.

🎉 GAMES AND 🎉 ACTIVITIES

Photo Shoot

You will need:

A camera

Film

Music to play ("Snapshot" by Ru Paul is perfect!)

What to do:

Now that everyone has been made up to look like a glamorous model, have a photo shoot! Turn on some up-beat music and tell the children to pose like models as you take pictures of them. After the party you could mail these pictures to your guests along with a thank you note. You could also take instant pictures with a Polaroid camera or use a digital camera and print them up on your computer to give to your guests as a party favor. Make sure that you get at least one or two photo shots of each child. When you run out of film just keep flashing for pretend.

Fashion Show

You will need:

Music to play (play songs like "The Catwalk" [various artists] or "Snapshot" [Ru Paul])

A spotlight or flashlights, optional

Toy microphone, optional

Information about the children to be read out loud (see Arrival of Guests), optional

Video camera, optional

What to do:

1. After everyone has been dressed up to look like a glamorous model, have a fashion show. Move all of your furniture out of the way to create a "runway" or pretend "catwalk" for the models to walk down. Seat ½ of the children on one side of the runway or catwalk and the other ½ on the other side. Give everyone a flashlight to shine as a spotlight on the "models" as they walk down the runway.

2. If you like, have a helper video-tape the models as they walk the pretend runway or catwalk. Begin playing some upbeat music and have one child at a time walk down the runway or catwalk. Let the birthday girl be the first to go up. Show her how to walk the runway before the party, so that the other children will know what to do. Give a brief description of each model's ensemble. If you have a toy microphone, use it to announce each child's name, age, a brief description of her hobbies and what school that she attends. This information can be written down by a helper as you are dressing the girls up. Make sure that everyone claps after each child is finished with her turn.

3. If time allows, show the children the video that you have taken.

Let's Go Shopping

You will need:

Magazines, newspaper inserts or store catalogues

Scissors

What to do:

1. Before the party, cut out pictures of beautiful outfits, shoes, purses and jewelry from the magazines, newspaper inserts or catalogues. Hide the pictures throughout the house or party area.

2. During the party, send the children "shopping" for the goods. The child to come back with the most pictures wins a prize, such as jewelry.

Memory Challenge

1. Seat all of the children in a circle. Begin by having the birthday child stand up in front of the group and slowly turn around in the center of the circle. Tell the other children to carefully observe the birthday child.

2. The birthday child then leaves the room and changes one thing about her appearance. She might put her hair in a ponytail, take it out of a ponytail, put on lipstick, take off a ring, move a ring to a different finger, move a bracelet from right wrist to left wrist, untie a shoelace, button a button, etc.

3. She then returns to the center of the circle and again turns around in the center of the circle. The other children must guess what has been changed. When someone guesses correctly, the birthday child goes back to her exact spot.

4. Moving in a clockwise direction, move on to the next child in the circle for her turn in the center of the circle. She does the same as the birthday child. Move on around the circle until everyone has had a turn.

Who's Got the Button?

You will need:

A large button
Music

1. Seat all of the children in a circle. Choose one child to go in the center of the circle.

2. Hand the button to one child in the circle.

3. As you begin playing the music, the children begin passing the button to one another behind their backs. All pretend to be grabbing the button, to confuse the child in the center of the circle.

4. Stop the music and tell the child in the center to guess who has the button. If she guesses correctly she wins a small prize, such as a piece of candy or an inexpensive ring.

5. Choose a different child to go into the center of the circle. Continue as before. Move around the circle in a clockwise direction, giving each child a turn in the center of the circle.

🎉 FAVOR AND 🎉 PRIZE IDEAS

Perfume, nail polish, play lipstick, nail stick-ons, stick-on stone earrings, costume jewelry, mirrors, combs, sunglasses, hair accessories, tiaras, photo albums, address books, candy necklaces, fresh flowers (see Decorations) Pasta Jewelry (see Crafts), Fancy Hats (see Crafts), Paper Plate Hats (see Crafts), photos of guests (see Activity "Photo Shoot") or picture frames.

Pirate Party

Ahoy there mate! So you're thinking about having a pirate party? Well, you're in for a treasure chest full of fun! What child isn't curious about pirates or fascinated by them? Your child and his shipmates will have a great time pretending that they are pirates searching for buried treasure, walking the plank and having their fortunes told at this swashbuckling affair.

Make this a costume party and ask your guests to come decked out in pirate-type clothing. Award a prize for the best costume.

Rent the movie "Treasure Island" and get to know some pirate lingo before the party. When your guests arrive, speak to them as a pirate would; you'll have them all in the spirit of the party.

I'll bet you'll have little landlubbers running around your neighborhood playing pirates for weeks after this party. We did!

🎉 TREASURE MAP 🎉 INVITATION

You can make an invitation that looks just like a real pirate's treasure map by following the directions below, or you can purchase printer paper that looks like a scroll at an office supply store and print this invitation on a computer printer. You could even print a picture of a pirate on your computer. If desired, write on the invitation, "Please wear pirate-type clothing."

You will need:

Brown paper bags
Matches or a lighter
A black felt tip marker or pen
Red ribbon or yarn

What to do:

1. Cut out a square from a brown paper bag, approximately 8 × 8 inches. You need one square per invitation.

2. Take the paper outdoors and singe the edges with a match or a lighter. Blow out the flames as you go. Only an adult must do this part of the invitation.

3. On the front of the invitation write your birthday invitation message. On the back draw a map (like a treasure map) to your home as illustrated (fig. 43).

4. Crumple the paper up a few times, opening it and crumpling again, to make it appear old and worn. This will soften the paper.

5. Roll the invitation up like a scroll and tie a ribbon or string around it to secure it. Have your child get all decked out in his or her pirate costume and hand-deliver the invitations to your guests, or fold the invitation up to mail it.

♟ DECORATIONS ♟

- Decorate the mailbox, front porch and party area with black, white and red balloons and crepe paper streamers.

- Make a sign that points to your house and reads "This way to buried treasure →." Put the sign next to your driveway or sidewalk.

- Put a plastic Halloween skeleton in your yard and place a pirate hat on him.

- Make a skull and crossbones flag for your front door with black construction paper for the flag background and white paper for the skull and crossbones.

- If you have a wooden toy box in your home, decorate it to look like a treasure chest. Place a large cardboard box inside of it as filler. Cover the box with a cloth or silky red material, such as a large scarf. Place plastic gold coins and costume jewelry on

(a)

(b)

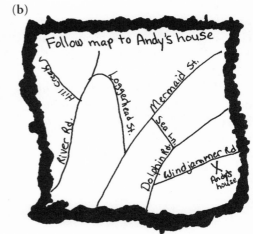

Fig. 43. Treasure Map Invitation

top of the material to make the treasure chest seem full of loot. Place this near your front door or in the party room.

- Suspend long balloon "swords" from the ceiling and give them to the children at the end of the party to have a sword fight the safe way.

- Make palm trees, anchors, boats, swords, fish, parrots and boat helms out of construction paper and hang them. Pictures such as these can also be purchased at a party supply store or printed on a computer printer.

- Use red, black and white for your tablecloth and tableware, or purchase pirate themed tableware.

- For a centerpiece, make a treasure chest from a cardboard box. Cover it with brown paper and cut black construction paper "leather" straps and a black lock. Wooden treasure boxes can also be purchased at craft stores and painted to look like a pirate's treasure box (this makes for a great play pretend treasure box after the party). Purchase gold plastic coins and spread them on the table along with some costume jewelry and metal goblets for loot. If you don't have metal goblets, you can make pretend ones by spray painting plastic disposable champagne glasses with glossy gold paint. Put some loot in the treasure box and make it hang out as if the box is overflowing with treasure. Give the loot away as party favors after the party. You could also use a model ship as a centerpiece and put seashells around it on the table, if you like.

- Play Caribbean steel band music or the song "Yo Ho (A Pirate's Life for

Me)" (Walt Disney Records, and the Official Album of Disneyland/Walt Disney World). If you have difficulty finding it in stores, you can order it by calling, Disney Merchandise at 1-800-272-6201. The mailing address is:

The Walt Disney Attractions
Guest Service/Mail Order Dept.
PO Box 10,070
Lake Buena Vista, Fl 32830-0070

🎉 FOOD 🎉

Tell the children that real pirates lived mostly off of fish (because it was plentiful), tough hard biscuits (to last on long journeys), limes (to prevent the disease scurvy) and salted meat (because it kept fresh on long journeys). The name buccaneer came from the French word "boucaner," the name of the smoking process when cooking meat, which left a distinctive aroma on the pirates.

Buccaneer Feast

- Tuna fish sandwiches

— or —

- Fried fish, fried shrimp or fish sticks served with tartar sauce or cocktail sauce.

- Biscuits (soft child-friendly biscuits, instead of the hard kind that pirates ate), if serving fish.

- Sword snacks: purchase sword shaped toothpicks (sometimes found in the mixed drink aisle of grocery stores) and spear them with chunks of fruit such as grapes, fresh orange slices, strawberries, pineapple, cantaloupe, watermelon, etc. Also spear separate skewers with mozzarella and cheddar cheese chunks.

- Real pirates drank rum, but this is obviously out of the question, so serve ginger ale or root beer. Place cans or bottles in a wooden barrel or tub filled with ice. You could also serve limeade or lemon lime soda.

Pirate Cake

You will need:

1 box of cake mix, plus ingredients as box directs

Heart shaped cake pan (found at kitchen and craft supply stores)

4 cups white frosting

Red and yellow food coloring

1 round 1½-inch diameter chocolate peppermint patty

Black shoestring licorice (found at candy stores)

Blue and red Fruit Roll-Ups or other fruit rolls

Several blue and one brown M & M

What to do:

1. Bake the cake and cool as directed. Cut the cake as shown in diagram (fig. 44a). If desired, freeze the cake pieces uncovered for about one hour to make the frosting spread more easily.

2. Remove the cake from the freezer and arrange on a platter or a foil-covered board as shown in diagram (fig. 44b).

3. Tint 3 cups of the frosting a flesh color, using a combination of pink icing and yellow icing. Frost the face and sides, being careful not to frost the top left side where the bandanna goes.

4. Tint the remaining frosting red and frost on the bandanna. Decorate the bandanna with blue candies.

5. Cut the licorice for hair and place it on the head to appear as if it is poking out from the bandanna.

6. Place the peppermint patty on the face for an eye patch and create a string for the eye patch using the shoestring licorice.

7. Cut a small circle out of the blue fruit roll for the inner eye. For the outline of the eye use licorice. Use the brown M & M candy for the pupil and attach with a dab of frosting.

8. Cut short pieces out of licorice for the eyebrows and beard stubble. Stick it into the frosting so that it points upward.

9. Cut a mouth shape from the red fruit roll and use a licorice strip for the divider on the lips.

10. For the nose and mustache use string licorice as shown in diagram (fig. 44b).

Note: Sometimes black shoestring licorice can be difficult to find. If you have difficulty finding it, you can substitute red licorice or black gel frosting, found in many grocery stores.

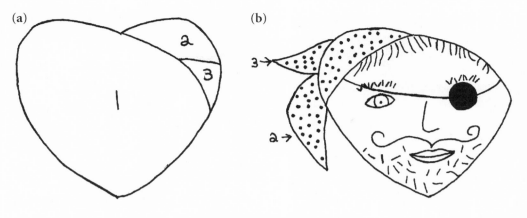

(a)   (b)

Fig. 44. Pirate Cake

Pirates on the Beach Cake

For a simple cake, frost one half of a sheet cake with butterscotch frosting or tan colored frosting as a beach. Frost the other half of the cake blue, and create waves by lifting the icing up. Place toy pirates, palm trees and a small treasure box on the beach. Stick a toy boat in the water and place a toy crocodile as if it were coming out of the water.

Treasure Cupcakes

This is a simple cake idea if you are short on time, or even if you need to make extra cake. Bake a batch of cupcakes and frost them blue. Place gold foil-wrapped chocolate coins on top and you're done! If desired, purchase pirate skull-and-crossbones flag toothpicks at a party supply store and stick one in each cupcake. If you can't find any, have your child make some out of 1 × 1½-inch pieces of black paper. Use white paper for the skull and crossbones and glue them to the flag. Poke the toothpick through the side of the flag. The birthday child might enjoy making these while you bake the cupcakes.

Treasure Chest Ice Cream

Put a scoop of ice cream on a paper cupcake liner. Use 4 square cookies such as graham crackers to form the box of the treasure chest around the scoop of ice cream. Place a 5th cookie in the ice cream, at the top, for the lid of the treasure chest. Use assorted candies, such as Jujyfruits or Dots, for jewels. Push gold foil-wrapped chocolate coins in the ice cream for gold coins.

🎉 ARRIVAL OF 🎉 GUESTS

As guests arrive, make them up to look like pirates, if they haven't already done it before they came. You will need someone to help you do this to speed things up. Ask the guests' parents if they mind if you put temporary tattoos on their children. They may be removed with baby oil, if anyone needs to be somewhere after the party. Also, ask if they mind if you put mustaches on their children with eyeliner. Give each child a thin mustache that is curled on the ends. Mustaches may be removed with make-up remover or cold cream. Purchase or make black eye patches for the children to wear. They won't wear them long, but it would be great to get everyone wearing their patches once for a picture. Black eye patches can be purchased at party supply stores and pharmacies. You can also make them out of black felt and black elastic. Give each child a nametag reading something like "Buccaneer Billy." Finish off the look by putting either a red bandanna or a pirate hat on each child. Now that everyone is all decked out to look like pirates, hand them a mirror to see how spiffy they look!

🎉 CRAFTS 🎉

Spyglasses

Since you will need plenty of paper towel rolls and toilet paper rolls for this craft, you will need to begin saving these well in advance. Ask a friend or relative to save some for you. Also, you need toilet paper tubes large enough for the paper towel tubes to fit inside. Some toilet paper tubes are narrower than others, so you may need to check the brand that you have before making these. If that's too much trouble, just use the paper towel tube without the toilet paper tubes.

You will need:

Empty cardboard paper towel tubes, 1 per telescope

Empty cardboard toilet paper tubes, 2 per telescope

Tape

9 × 12-inch sheets of brown construction paper, 1 per telescope

1½ × 6-inch pieces of black construction paper, 3 per telescope

Glue

What to do:

1. Tape the two toilet paper tubes together end to end.

2. Fold the 9 × 12-inch sheet of brown paper in half. Cut it to make two 6 × 9-inch sheets.

3. Run glue along each 9-inch end of both sheets. Attach one sheet to the two toilet paper tubes and the other to the paper towel tube. About 1½ inches of the paper towel tube will remain exposed.

4. Run glue along the 1½-inch end of each black strip of construction paper. Attach one black strip to the exposed end of the paper towel tube. Attach the other two strips to the brown paper of the toilet paper tubes, attaching one strip on each end.

5. Insert the end of the paper towel tube that does not have a black strip on it into the inside of the two toilet paper tubes. It may be tight at first, so you may need to work it in. The tubes will slide back and forth like the parts of a telescope. You now have a telescope ready for spotting pirate ships!

Treasure Chest Boxes

Give each child a shoebox or a small cardboard box and let the children decorate them as treasure chests. Cover a table with some newspaper or a paper tablecloth to protect it and put out some construction paper, scissors, glue, felt tip markers, plastic craft gems, sequins and beads. Let the children be creative with their designs. Put their names on their boxes and use them for a treasure hunt or as a favor holder.

🎉 GAMES AND 🎉 ACTIVITIES

Gypsy Fortune Teller

For this activity, you will need to tell the children a future prediction or a fortune. You can use the listed predictions below, but to make the fortunes more personal and exciting, ask the parents what their child wants to be when they grow up. You can ask this question as the parents call to RSVP. Ask them not to let their child hear the conversation, if possible. Write the answers down on a list next to each guest's name. If your child knows what his friends want to be when they grow up, he can help you with this list also. When the child goes to have their fortune told they will be amazed that the prediction is what they had really hoped for. This makes it more exciting for them.

You will need:

A crystal ball: a round vase or a bowl turned upside down, possibly even a glass ball paperweight

A small table covered with a silky red or dark colored tablecloth

Two chairs

A candle, optional (use this only if an adult will be giving the fortunes)

Black light bulbs, optional

An adult or child dressed as a gypsy: wear a head scarf tied at the side, a long skirt with a scarf tied over the hip, long fake nails, large round earrings and gaudy costume jewelry.

A tent: use a real tent or make a tent from a cloth tarp or large black plastic tarp (found at a hardware store), optional.

A list of fortunes given from parents, or see the following list:

> You will be very rich
> You will be a famous baseball player
> You will get many A's on your next report card
> You will be very handsome/ beautiful when you grow up
> You are a great painter and will grow up to be an artist
> You are a great singer and will grow up to be a musician

What to do:

1. Before the party, set up the table with a tablecloth draped over it in a room or in a tent. Put the candle and the "crystal ball" on the table. Set two chairs next to the table, one on

each side. If possible close the curtains or the tent flaps to create a mysterious look. Place the list of fortunes under the table. If desired, and if setting up in a separate room, change the light bulbs to give an interesting effect.

2. During the party, light the candle, if using one. Have one person stand outside of the room or the tent and let you know who will be entering, so that you may read the child's fortune from the list before they enter. Call one guest in at a time.

3. As the child enters the room, talk with an accent as a gypsy would talk. Ask the child to take a seat. Rub your crystal ball and pretend that the ball is sending you a vision. Give the child a fortune. Continue until each child has had a turn.

Variation: Place written fortunes inside of a glass vase or glass bowl and have the children "draw" a fortune from the vase. For example the fortune could say, "You will win a ring in the near future" or "You will win an eye patch in the near future." The fortune that the child draws is the prize that he will receive.

Hunt for the Birthday Present

Have a treasure hunt with the birthday gifts. The children giving the gifts must hide them around the house and the birthday child must find them before opening them.

X Marks the Spot

Hang a treasure map on a wall, door or refrigerator. Hand each child an "X" made out of black construction paper, with a loop of tape stuck onto the back, and his name written on the front with white crayon or white correction fluid. Line the children up. Have each child take a turn at being blindfolded with a bandanna and trying to stick the "X" onto a picture of a treasure chest drawn on the map. The one who comes the closest wins.

Treasure Hunt

Now what would a pirate party be without a good old fashioned treasure hunt? Hide a treasure box full of children's costume jewelry and gold chocolate or plastic coins (use plastic in hot weather, the chocolate will melt). Make treasure maps out of brown paper bags, just like the invitations for this party. Make one treasure map for each group of children. Have about 4 children in each group. Draw a map of your yard that includes everything in your yard. Don't leave out even the tiniest details. Write clues up in one corner of the map, but make the clues different for each map. Have the maps sending each group off in different direction at the start of the hunt. One group's map could have clues sending them to the newspaper box to look for the next clue. When they get to the newspaper box, have a clue hidden inside of the newspaper box, which sends them to the outdoor cooking grill for the next clue, etc. Some great places to hide clues are: under a doormat, under a flower pot, under a garbage can, under a recycle bin, under a picnic table, under a chair, behind a bush, by a wood pile, under a rock, etc. For parties with older children, you can make the clues more difficult by writing on the hidden slips of paper something like, "Take ten paces north (ten giant steps north) and turn right until you get to the large tree. Look for the next clue near the large tree." You could call a crawl space under the house "the bat cave" and suspend Halloween bats from the entrance door with fishing line. Call a pond "Mermaid Lagoon" or a landscaped area "Treasure Island." Make sure that all of the maps lead to the same treasure, and are equal in the amount and type of clues given. The group who finds the treasure first wins, but all share the loot inside!

Cannonball Throw

You will need:

A hula-hoop

String or rope

Two balls or toy bowling balls (preferably black to resemble cannonballs)

What to do:

1. Before the party, hang the hula-hoop from a tree branch, a basketball hoop or a ceiling.

2. During the party, line the children up single file behind a marked spot that is about 10–12 feet from the hula-hoop. Allow each child 3 throws at the hula-hoop. Any child to get 2 balls through the hoop wins a prize.

Variation: Hang a toy boat or shark so that it hangs down at the center of the hoop. Any child to hit the toy boat or shark once wins a prize.

Ship Shoot

You will need:

1 empty plastic 2 liter soda bottle

Approximately ⅓–½ cup of sand or dirt

A craft knife

One wooden bamboo skewer, for the ship mast

½ sheet of typing paper cut crosswise to resemble the ship sail

Tape

1 wallpaper water tray (found at hardware stores) or any long narrow tray, filled ½ full with water

A chair

A cork gun, foam dart gun or plastic dart gun

What to do:

1. Before the party, fill the plastic bottle with just enough dirt or sand to hold the sail upright. Place the bottle on its side.

2. Poke a tiny hole in the side of the bottle, near the middle of the bottle. It should only be wide enough for the skewer to fit through. Push the skewer in the hole until it stops.

3. Tape the paper sail to the mast. Now the bottle is your ship. Place it into the tray of water.

4. During the party, set the tray, with the ship floating in it, onto a table (a picnic table would be perfect). Set the chair 6–7 feet away from the ship.

5. Line the children up behind the chair and give each child 3 shots of the gun at the ship. The children may use the back of a chair as a gun rest. Any child who hits the boat at least one time wins a prize, or if you like, award a prize to the child who hits it the most times.

Walk the Plank

You will need:

An 8-foot-long wood 2 × 4 (for parties with children 6 and under, use a 1 × 6)
Plastic toy sharks and fish, or sharks cut out of gray construction paper
A blindfold

What to do:

Place the "plank" on a level floor or ground. Blindfold the children and have them take turns walking from one end of the plank to the next. An adult will need to stay close to the children as they walk across, just in case they should lose their balance. Award a prize to anyone making it across the board without falling off. All will think that it is going to be an easy win, but they are in for a surprise! An appropriate prize would be a toy shark or fish from around the plank.

Note: Do not blindfold small children. Just let them walk across.

Man Overboard

See Fishing Party.

Cannonball Toss

See Pool and Beach Party game "Water Balloon Toss." Play with black balloons.

Hot Cannonball

You will need:

1 ball (black if possible)
Caribbean-style music

What to do:

Seat all of the children in a circle on the floor or ground. Hand the ball to one of the children in the circle. Start the music. As the music begins the children pass the ball around the circle clockwise. When the music stops, the child caught holding the ball is out of the game, but receives a token prize, such as a piece of candy. The music begins again and the children continue passing the ball. This continues until two children are left. The child not stuck with the ball is the winner.

Pirate's Cave

Cover a card table with a blanket, leaving one end open. Place gold foil-wrapped chocolate coins on the floor of the "cave." As each child comes out of the game Hot Cannonball he may go into the cave for a piece of gold.

Pirate Piñata

See the chapter on piñatas (end of book).

One Legged Relay

You will need:

Two balls (preferably black)

What to do:

1. Divide the children into two equal teams, and line them up single file behind a marked starting line. Set a marked goal line for the children to run to.

2. Hand one ball to the first child in each line. At the signal to go, the children must hop to the goal and back on one leg, holding the ball at the same time. They pass the ball off to the next child in line who does the same. The first team to have all of its members finish first wins.

FAVOR AND PRIZE IDEAS

Bandannas, pirate hats (felt or cardboard), eye patches, plastic gold coins, gold foil-wrapped chocolate coins, temporary tattoos, toy telescopes or spyglasses (see Crafts), kaleidoscopes, plastic boats, plastic fish, stick-on mustaches, clip-on ring earrings, costume jewelry, compasses, toy swords, balloon swords, plastic pirate figures, beef jerky, gummy fish, saltwater taffy or cannonball candy (malted milk balls). You can even make cardboard swords by cutting cardboard into a sword shape and covering it with aluminum foil and black construction paper.

Piñatas

Where the piñata (peen-ya-tah) originated is uncertain. Some historians believe that it originated in pre–Columbian times, while others believe that it comes from China or Italy. Whatever the case may be, piñatas have been enjoyed by millions of people around the world for over 400 years.

Traditionally piñatas were used to celebrate a good harvest. They were made of clay and filled with fruits and vegetables. Today they are made of newspaper, cardboard and a flour mixture. The treats put in a piñata represent good wishes and the person that breaks open the piñata is thought to have good luck all through the coming year.

At all of the birthday parties in my home and at some of our holidays and school events we have a piñata for the children. A birthday party in my neighborhood just wouldn't be the same without a piñata. All of the children that are regulars at our parties have come to expect them, and if there isn't one they are disappointed and want to know why. I almost always make my own, but I have had to buy a couple when time was short. I think that one of the great things about having a piñata is that it not only makes for an excellent game, but it doubles as a decoration. Your guests are going to love these!

PAPIER-MÂCHÉ RECIPE AND PIÑATA BASE DIRECTIONS

You can purchase papier-mâché (pa-per ma-SHAY) in a powdered form at arts and crafts stores. I prefer to make my own. Do not try to double or triple the recipe. Most piñatas are done in several stages, drying between stages, and will not require a lot of paste for each stage done. It is hard to save, so make more paste as you need it.

You will need:

1 cup of flour

¾ cup of warm tap water

Medium bowl (use an old bowl)

Large bowl (use an old bowl)

Newspaper

A mold: use an inflated balloon in the shape preferred, a rounded bowl, or an inverted pie dish

Waxed paper, if using the bowl or pie dish as a mold

Cardboard for added features: toilet paper tubes, paper towel tubes, the back of a notepad, etc., optional

A wire coat hanger

Duct tape

Piñata filler: soft well wrapped candy, toys, trinkets, shelled peanuts, several filled small lunch bags, etc.

What to do:

1. Place the inflated balloon (if using) inside the large bowl, to hold it in place while you work on it. If using a bowl or a pie dish as a mold, turn it upside down and cover it with waxed paper to keep the papier-mâché from sticking to it. Fold the waxed paper under the rim, to hold it in place.

2. Pour the flour into the medium bowl. Add water and stir. Remove all the lumps with a spoon or by squeezing the paste between your hands (remove any jewelry you may be wearing). The paste should feel smooth, with a cream-like consistency, and somewhat like glue. It should not be thick like pudding.

3. Tear the newspaper along the edge of a countertop or a squared surface. It is best to tear the newspaper vertically. If you tear horizontally it is difficult to tear. Do not cut the newspaper. The rougher edges caused from tearing the newspaper adhere better. The strips should be about 1 inch wide and 5 or 6 inches long. Do not use colored newspaper, if you will be using light colored tissue paper to cover the piñata, and if you feel it will show through.

4. Dip one strip of newspaper into the flour mixture at a time. Do not allow the newspaper to sit in the flour mixture and become too saturated, or it will tear. Hold it up with one hand and gently squeeze out the excess flour mixture with two fingers of the other hand.

5. Place the strips over the balloon or mold, one at a time. Put the strips on unevenly or in a criss-cross fashion. Try not to put too many on top of one another, or it will take a longer time to dry. Leave a space for a hole to put the candy or goodies in. Where you leave a space will depend on the position the piñata will hang from. Check the instructions in this chapter for each piñata.

6. Dry completely between layers. The piñata may be set outside to dry in warm dry weather. This speeds drying tremendously, but temperatures above 80° may cause balloons to ex-

pand and pop. You may need to dry it overnight in most cases.

7. The piñata must be completely dry before adding more layers. Add 2 or 3 layers for small children. As children get older, they get stronger, and it may be necessary to strengthen the piñata with 5 or 6 layers. If you will be using two half molds to create one mold, it would be at this time that you would fill the molds with goodies and insert a wire coat hanger between the two molds for hanging (see step 9 for further instructions). Connect the two molds with one or two layers of papier-mâché. It is also at this time that you would add any features with cardboard or shaped newspaper (e.g., legs, arms, nose, ears, etc.). Use papier-mâché to attach the features.

8. When all of the layers have dried, pop the balloon (if using) with a pin, remove and discard it.

9. Shape a wire coat hanger to fit inside of the piñata (this will become the piñata hanger). Use pliers to turn the hook of the coat hanger inward so that no sharp points will be sticking out. Make a hanging loop with the hook of the coat hanger. Cover any sharp points with duct tape.

10. Stuff the piñata with ¾ of the chosen filler, setting some aside for children who do not get enough. If necessary, stuff the opening of the piñata with crumbled newspaper to give the opening the proper shape when you seal it closed. Seal shut by wrapping more papier-mâché around the coat hanger (for added strength) and over the opening.

11. After the piñata has completely dried, decorate according to the instructions in the following pages for each piñata or decorate as you wish. If you like, take colored strips of tissue paper cut 2–3 inches wide, fold in half and cut slits at the unfolded edge to resemble fur. Glue the strips to the piñata, working from the bottom of the piñata to the top. Use construction paper for features. Yarn can be used for hair or mustaches. Disposable bowls can be used for hats.

12. To use the piñata, see Hanging and Breaking instructions at the end of this chapter.

Variation: Some people like to use rope instead of the wire coat hanger to hang the piñata. If you prefer to use rope, it must be tied around the mold or placed inside of the piñata with a loop exposed, and held in place with a few layers of papier-mâché. You can anchor the rope in place by tying it around an unsharpened pencil or a wooden dowel. Place it inside of the piñata and pull up on it. Then close the hole with papier-mâché, wrapping some papier-mâché around the pencil or dowel to secure it. If you do use rope, make sure that you use rope that is strong enough to hold the weight of the piñata when it is filled with all of its goodies.

Variation: If you like, stuff the piñata with zippered plastic bags labeled with each child's name on one bag. This would ensure that everyone would get the same amount of goodies and keep the goodies clean at the same time.

🎉 BEEHIVE 🎉 PIÑATA

This piñata is very simple to make. Follow the Piñata Base Directions, using a balloon for the mold. When the piñata is completely dry, wrap brown or tan crepe paper around it horizontally and glue or tape in place. If desired, make bees out of yellow construction paper. Use a black felt tip marker to draw lines, a stinger and eyes on each bee. Glue the bees to the beehive. See illustration (fig. 45).

Fig. 45. Beehive Piñata

🎉 DINOSAUR 🎉 PIÑATA

Follow the Piñata Base Directions, using a balloon for the mold. Use 4 toi-

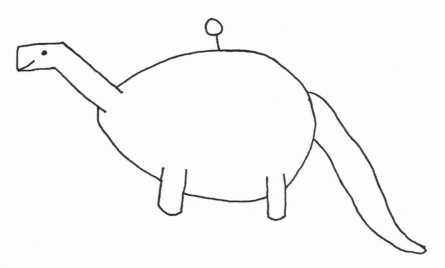

Fig. 46. Dinosaur Piñata

let paper rolls for the legs, and cut a few ¾-inch slits on each. Spread out the slits to make a base. This will help the legs stay on better. Attach the legs with one layer of papier-mâché strips, both inside of the leg and outside. Use a paper towel roll for the neck and head, putting it on the same way as the legs, and bend it at the top to form the head. Crumple a piece of newspaper to form the tail, and attach with one layer of papier-mâché strips. Allow it to dry completely. Paint the piñata green and use a sponge to add touches of brown paint to the body. See illustration (fig. 46).

🎉 PIG PIÑATA 🎉

Follow the Piñata Base Directions, using a balloon for the mold. Use 4 toilet paper rolls for the legs, and cut a few ¾-inch slits on each. Spread out the slits to make a base. This will help the legs stay on better. Attach the legs with one layer of papier-mâché strips, both inside and outside of the leg. Make a snout by attaching a cut yogurt cup or a disposable cup with one layer of papier-mâché strips. Completely dry all layers. Wrap the piñata with pink crepe paper, gluing where necessary, or paint the piñata with pink acrylic paint. Cut two ears out of pink construction paper and glue them on. Draw on a mouth with black felt tip marker or cut one out of black paper. Cut two white circles out of paper for the eyes, and glue two smaller black circles on top for the pupils. Use curled pink wrapping paper ribbon for the tail, or cut a spiral out of a circle of

pink construction paper. (To make a spiral out of paper, start the cut on the outside edge of the paper and keep cutting around and around until you get to the center.) See illustration (fig. 47)

Fig. 47. Pig Piñata

🎉 PIRATE PIÑATA 🎉

This piñata will require more work than most in this chapter. Follow the Piñata Base Directions, using one regular size balloon for the body and one small balloon for the head. When placing the papier-mâché on the small balloon, leave a hole at the top and a hole at the bottom of the balloon. It will not be necessary to fill this small mold with goodies. When you make the large piñata, make the hanger or rope long enough so that it will be able to fit through the holes of the small piñata (the "head"). Attach the head to the body with more papier-mâché and seal any openings. Use 4 paper towel rolls for arms and legs. Cut the arms shorter than the legs and bend up one end of each leg to form the feet. Attach all 4 pieces to the body by cutting ¾-inch slits on one end of each, spreading out the slits and holding them in place with a layer of papier-mâché strips. Make a nose by cutting a piece of cardboard in a triangle shape. Bend it in half and attach it with papier-mâché strips. Allow the piñata to dry. Paint on a red and white striped shirt, black pants that come just past the "knee" (with jagged edges), black shoes, flesh colored legs and face, a red mouth, a black eyepatch, and a black outline for one eye. Fill the eye outline in with white paint and paint on a blue or brown circle with a black pupil. Make one hand out of cardboard and paint it flesh colored with black lines for fingers. Stick the hand in the end of one arm. Make a cardboard hand hook and cover it with aluminum foil. Stick the hook in the other arm. Make a mustache out of black yarn, laying several layers on top of one another. Tie them at the center with another piece of yarn. Glue the mustache on over the

mouth, allowing it to hang down over the mouth. Finish off your pirate with a real bandanna on his head. See illustration (fig. 48).

🎉 HANGING 🎉 THE PIÑATA

There are many ways to hang the piñata and everyone has his own idea of how it should be done. The type of yard or area that you have to hang it really will determine where and how it will be hung. Keep in mind that wherever you hang your piñata it must be away from light fixtures or other breakable objects. You will want to keep it out of the direct sunlight if it is filled with candy that will melt easily. Hang the piñata just before your guests are to arrive. If the ground below the piñata is dirty, spread out a large tarp to keep the candy clean. The area under and around the piñata should be clean and free of objects that might hurt the children. Below are some ways that you may choose to hang the piñata:

Version 1: Tie a rope between 2 trees. From the center of that rope securely tie another rope. Tie the piñata to the end of the hanging rope. The piñata should hang just above the head of the average guest's height.

Version 2: Tie a rope between 2 trees. Tie another rope to the piñata and throw that rope over the suspended rope. You will be able to raise or lower the piñata as you choose with this method by holding the rope at the opposite end of the piñata. This

Fig. 48. Pirate Piñata

method works well for parties with children of different heights.

Version 3: For this version, you don't hang the piñata from a permanent support; instead, an adult will hold the piñata up as the children swing. Take a stick, such as an old broomstick, and drill a hole through one end. String a rope through one end and tie it tight. At the other end of the rope tie the piñata. Now you simply hold the piñata up by the broomstick. As with version 2, you will be able to raise or lower the piñata as you choose. Just stay clear of the swinging bat. You may want to use a lightweight 18-inch piñata bat for this version.

Version 4: Hang the piñata from a sturdy joist in your basement. Keep the piñata within a safe swinging distance away from any poles, light fixtures, or other objects.

Version 5: If it rains and you are forced to bring the party indoors, but you do not have a basement, consider your garage. If you have a beam that is not covered with drywall, hang the piñata from it. One year we were forced to bring our party indoors because it rained. The only place that we had to hang our piñata was between the garage door metal runners. Our runners are strong and very sturdy. Check yours to see if they too are sturdy. If you also must resort to this method, hang your rope from the strongest point, usually the far top end, near the brackets that support the runners.

Version 6: Hang a rope from a very strong tree branch (one that extends out and well away from its trunk), and at the other end hang the piñata.

Version 7: At one time I lived in a house that had no place to hang a piñata. The one tree in the yard had weak limbs. We had no basement and no garage. The only place that we could hang the piñata — a piñata we were determined to use! — was from the wooden porch railing that was high above the ground. (This of course was before we found out about version 3.) I don't like to suggest this one, because it could damage your porch, but if you happen to be planning to replace your porch railings, then it will be fine. You will need to drill a hole into an 8-foot wooden 2×4. Extend the 2×4 out from the porch railing, far enough so that the children can swing without hitting anything, and hammer the board into the top of the railing. Hang the rope from the drilled hole and tie the piñata to the other end of the rope.

⚝ BREAKING ⚝ THE PIÑATA

Keep in mind that some, not all, store-bought piñatas may break easily, and if you put too many layers on a homemade piñata it may be very difficult to break open. If your homemade one is very strong, you may need to use a baseball bat to break the piñata, since a broomstick may break and fly off into the air, creating a dangerous situation. Some people like to use a broomstick, but I do not. I feel that they are not strong enough.

As your guests arrive, warn them not to swing at the piñata until you say to. You will need to keep a close eye on some children, because they *will* try to, unless you have a group of angels.

You will need:

A blindfold: a bandanna, a scarf, or even a large adult hat placed so that it covers the eyes

A baseball bat or a piñata bat (if it is sturdy)

Goody holders: paper lunch bags, plastic goody bags, baskets, or buckets (labeled with names)

What to do:

1. Line all of the children up in a half circle around the piñata at a *very* safe swinging distance. Place the birthday child first, then all of the smaller children and then biggest children last. You will definitely need to keep the strongest children at the end of the line, but explain to them that your reason for this is because they have such big muscles. Inflate their egos, so that they don't get irritated about being at the back of the line at every one of your parties. If you don't do this, the piñata will be broken before anyone ever gets a turn to swing at the piñata. Hand each child his container for holding his goodies.

2. Blindfold the birthday child. Place his container nearby so that he will be able to reach it if the piñata should break (or an adult can hold it and be ready to pass it to him).

3. Turn him around 3 times to throw off his sense of direction, but not wildly. Hand him the stick or baseball bat, and get everyone, including yourself, out of his way. You may need to remind some children to stay back. Tell the birthday child to try and hit the piñata. If you only have a few guests, and the children are 7 and younger, allow 2 or 3 swings. If you have a lot of children attending the party, or the children are older, only allow 1 swing at the piñata. Cheer on the person up to bat.

4. If he breaks the piñata and the goodies fall to the ground, then tell all of the children that they may scramble for the candy. Make sure that the hitter removes his bandanna and gets his container. Take the bat away from the hitter so that no one gets hit in the rush.

5. If the first child doesn't break the piñata, then the next child in line gets a turn. This continues until someone breaks the piñata.

6. Sometimes the piñata will crack a little and a few items will fall out. All of the children are sure to scramble for the pieces, but tell them to stop and wait. Explain to them that it will need to be hit more to fully break it open. Continue playing, if necessary.

7. Sometimes there will be a few pieces left in the piñata. Either throw them toward the floor or ground or give them to a child who didn't get enough. Now would also be a good time to

give any children your reserved goodies. Go around and look in everyone's containers to see who didn't get much. Make sure you slip some goodies in their containers or point out things on the floor or ground that they have missed. This prevents any hurt feelings.

8. After all of the goodies have been picked up, ask the children to help pick up the broken piñata pieces and toss them in the trash. This will prevent the children from throwing them all over and making a mess of your yard or house. It would also be a good idea to remove the remaining piñata from the rope and throw it away. The children are sure to use it for batting practice, which could hurt someone. Also, put the bat away at this time.

Index